From Winning Teams

to Broken Dreams

The story of six friends and their journey to

reach the Premier League

From Winning Teams to Broken Dreams

The story of six friends and their journey to reach the Premier League

Dominic Ball

ISBN – 979 8 80063 705 2

Cover design by Brendan McMahon of Classic Lines Design

Edited by Chris Green.

DEDICATION

This book is dedicated to the memory of Spencer McCall, one of the six lads featured in this book.

All author royalties from the sales of this book will go to Sarcoma UK, which is a national charity that funds vital research, offers support for anyone affected by sarcoma cancer and campaigns for better treatment.

It is the only UK cancer charity focusing on sarcomas, which are uncommon cancers that can affect any part of the body, on the inside or outside, including the muscle, bone, tendons, blood vessels and fatty tissues. 15 people are diagnosed with sarcoma every day in the UK, some 5,300 people a year.

Sarcoma UK relies on generous voluntary donations and the energy and imagination of the charity's tireless fundraisers. The charity has invested over £4.2 million into 63 high quality scientific research projects and has helped more than 1,400 people through the free and confidential Support Line which was launched in February 2016.

For further information see https://sarcoma.org.uk.

Table of Contents

ACKNOWLEDGEMENTS

It has taken five years for me to write this book and I'm excited to be sharing it with everyone.

It has changed drastically over this period and a first massive thank you goes to Chris Green for making this a reality. Chris shared my vision for the book and along with his knowledge, patience and writing ability he has helped to make this experience a special one. Without Chris this wouldn't have been possible and he has been amazing to work with. Thank you so much Chris.

Secondly, I would like to thank those most important to me for all the support throughout my life and career.

None of this would have been possible without Mum and Dad. I cannot thank you enough for the love, support and opportunities you have provided me with both on and off the pitch, the teachings and values you have instilled in me and everything else you have given me in anything I've decided to do in my life. As always, I hope that this book makes you feel proud.

Also, to my brothers, Matt, Phil and Abel who have lived this journey with me the whole way. Thank you so much for the support, honesty, and encouragement you have given me. I hope that I am as helpful to you guys as you are to me.

To Jess, my amazing fiancée who now knows every little thing about the world of football having read this book a dozen times or more. Thank you for being there every step of the way and especially during the turbulent times when I know it must have been difficult. You are amazing and I am so grateful to have you by my side.

To the group of lads mentioned in this book. Thank you for being a part of this book which will hopefully raise a lot of money for a great cause and to raise awareness of the difficult footballing journey. Sharing all our stories can be tough so thank you for your willingness to share your experiences and for being honest about your journeys. We are truly lucky to have the group of friends that we do.

Lastly, I would like to thank the coaches that have helped me along the way. Although a lot of my education was on the pitch, these coaches also provided me with important life lessons. At Spurs I would like to thank John McDermott, Alex Inglethorpe, Kieran McKenna, Matt Wells, Chris Ramsey, Les Ferdinand, and Tim Sherwood. I am so lucky to have had these top coaches in the developmental stages of my career.

To all the Watford coaches who welcomed me into academy football. Special thanks in particular to Nick Cox, who worked with me on a daily basis for four years and helped me improve significantly.

To the managers that have helped me on my journey and had to deal with me in my good and bad, which you will find out more about in the book, thank you – especially Mark Warburton who provided me with great opportunities both at Glasgow Rangers and Queens Park Rangers, Paul Warne who has always been very honest with me, Derek McInnes who helped me rediscover my love for football and the importance of winning and to Grant McCann for the opportunity at Peterborough.

Finally thank you to Jag Shoker who has been an influential mentor to me throughout the whole process. Thank you for all of the hard work, guidance and honesty you have provided.

FOREWORD - CHRIS GREEN

From *Winning Teams to Broken Dreams* is an important book for many reasons.

For starters, it is being published to raise money for Sarcoma UK, which funds research and offers support for people affected by sarcoma cancer which sadly took the life of one of the young men featured in this book, Spencer McCall.

Secondly, as a journalist who has looked in depth at football youth development and the English football academy system over the past three decades, Dominic Ball gives voice to those who should always matter most – the boys who give their all to become professional footballers.

When asked to edit this book, I was struck by how often the varying emotions expressed by these young men are so routinely drowned out by vested interests, wishful thinkers, serial deniers and ill-informed journalists.

To his immense credit, Dominic Ball has managed to write this book in mid-career while competing in the most challenging of professional sports, not least the highly demanding English Football League Championship, the second tier of English football with its relentless 46 games per season. Crucially it has been written while the experiences recalled are still raw with emotion and fresh in the minds of Dom and his friends.

Like all the boys featured in this book, who are equally lucid in recalling their experiences, Dom was plucked from the bonhomie of junior football to compete in the serious business of Premier League academy football. Without needing to sensationalise their stories, this book describes what thousands of academy boys go through during childhood to pursue their dream of becoming professional footballers. It is also a tale of their parents, siblings and coaches too.

That none of the lads featured in this book has achieved the dream of playing Premier League football isn't down to a lack of effort but fate and fortitude in the sheer weight of competition and overwhelming statistical odds.

This is their story – the flesh and bone feelings behind those broken dreams.

INTRODUCTION

KICKABOUTS

I'm 21 years old and sat with my best mates sipping beer around the patio table at our family home in a quiet country village on the northern outskirts of London.

I spent my childhood in this house and have many fantastic memories of growing up here. I love the large garden, with a patio overlooking grass, swings and a pear tree cascading down to a mini football pitch at the foot of the garden.

Having three soccer mad boys, my dad, who helped to run a good local junior club and played non-League football to a decent level himself, built three-metre-high fences on either side to prevent balls careering into neighbouring gardens which led to understandable complaints.

With tall laurel bushes at the rear to block our view of a distant quarry and the fields beyond, it is effectively surrounded on three sides so, to me at least, resembles a caged five-a-side pitch.

The meticulous layout was the only tell-tale sign that the seemingly typical early 20-something aged mates enjoying a beer, barbecue, and back garden kickabout had a bit more interest than most in the so-called 'beautiful game'.

A couple of the lads have already put on a bit too much timber for their age to fully enjoy an energetic ad hoc game – but with beer and burgers in our bellies none of us seem up for it anyway.

Among our number were three former academy players - Beau, a qualified carpenter, Jack, who designs and fits luxury sheds, and Mason, an electrician. Three of us had progressed to being professional footballers. Spencer is a semi-pro local league player, Lawrence a goalie for a League Two club and I was playing in League One back then.

So why didn't we fancy a kickabout given that is what half of us did for a living?

Too much of a busman's holiday for those earning a crust as professional footballers? For the lads no longer playing, perhaps the game itself served as a recent uncomfortable reminder of what might have been? Maybe our love of the game had just waned too much?

You see, we'd all met through football. Not as mates who'd enjoyed a kickabout in the park you understand or lads who played for the same school team but as boys competing at England's top-flight football academies.

Our dream was every boy's dream - not just to become professional footballers but *Premier League* players – household names on everyone's lips, stars that lit up the most prestigious league in world football. Scorers of amazing goals. Three Lions on our international jerseys and fabulously wealthy too, of course, beyond our wildest dreams with supermodel girlfriends, sports cars and other trappings of the rich and famous.

We were good. Oh yes, we were all good alright. Not just as boys with potential but the supposed chosen few who had been spotted and signed at primary school age and spirited away to train and play in the opulent facilities on offer at England's top club academies.

Not for us muddy parks pitches or dilapidated schools' facilities run by willing workers or over stressed schoolteachers. Only the best would do, be it pristine pitches, fourth generation artificial surfaces that mimic real grass or state-of-the-art gyms kitted out with the latest fitness tracking devices and feverishly monitored by sports scientists and physicians working alongside specialist youth coaches whose sole role was to hone us into football stars of the future.

We were pampered too. We wore club apparel, were ferried by taxi to and from school, taken to away games on luxury coaches and had education and welfare officers looking after our pastoral needs. We didn't overplay – no congested schools, district, county or recreational football schedule to tire us out. We competed exclusively for the professional clubs we had joined.

We also shared the same facilities as the first team stars we aspired to become. With dedication and a fair wind, each of us stood a realistic chance of living the dream that their lives had become. It was within tantalising distance. We could see, hear, smell and almost touch it.

Only, as this book explains, it isn't as simple as that. Huge questions have been asked about the way football recruits and develops young talent – not least why the process now starts at such an alarmingly young age, with boys recruited often as young as four or five years of age by professional clubs. Aside from the practicalities and unpredictability involved, there are ethical dilemmas wrapped around such a hard-bitten, competitive process which frequently results in young people succumbing to its pressures in the shadow of shattered dreams.

So, there we all were – 21 or 22-year-olds, football's once chosen few, now too bored or jaded to even participate in the most rudimentary of back garden kickabouts.

Where did it all go wrong?

Six years earlier, same garden, same set of lads it had all been so different.

As eager 15-year-olds, sporting shirts, shorts and socks stained with sweat and grass, the barbecue provided mere sustenance to be washed down with lashings of squash to quench our thirsts between games we'd meticulously organised to entertain ourselves all day. We just couldn't get enough of it.

You see, football back then was still about fun - the single factor that brought us together from different parts of London and the surrounding suburbs despite the awkward logistics involved - a net cast far beyond the geographical confines of most kids of our age. The allure of football was enough and the reason we'd spent so much time playing it virtually from the time we had learned to stand up straight.

We had an insatiable appetite for the game. The excitement of testing and challenging our skills filled our senses. We revelled in the thrill of showing off in the self-devised games we'd set to make the whole day's footy interesting, relevant and fun.

Although we had wider circles of friends we'd met through football, it was somehow this group of mates that magically became a closer band of brothers, even though many of us played for different clubs and were often at different levels of our development.

From the age of nine, our weekends would see us play anywhere in the country, sporting shirts belonging to the biggest clubs in England. If you think the meticulous preparation that enables this to happen is just for fun you're living in dreamland. If you believe, as many do, that the end always justifies the means and there is no undue pressure involved for the participants, be they children or parents, then I'm afraid this book is about to shatter some myths.

The harsh reality of the football business (for that is what it is – a business) was still to hit home as we enjoyed that warm summer day in 2010. Although we played back garden football many times, that day belonged to us, a special moment ahead of the most critical year of our lives (would we, wouldn't we be offered a scholarship – the must-achieve route to becoming a professional player for 16-18-year-olds). It was a timely reminder of why we loved football so much. Our rules, our way, for our enjoyment - and it was magical. A truly treasured memory that will stay with me and the other lads forever. Forever.

The day began with a keepy-uppy game of two-touch or one-touch one-bounce, which requires close skill far beyond the ability of most 15-year-olds but reasonably easy for proficient players like us which meant we kept it going for an hour or more.

Not that we were in a hurry. Football was everything and this competitive knock-out game meant you had a number of 'lives' and were eliminated when you lost them all resulting in an ignominious forfeit - typically an ear flick (a resounding flick of the forefinger to your ear from each of your mates – painful, but strangely funny) or a bum slap, which requires the loser to stand facing the other way as each player in turn tries to thunder the ball at your backside from a distance of 10 yards - a jokey game that is commonplace in football.

Next was head tennis. We split into two evenly matched teams with a five-a-side sized goal frame acting as an ad hoc net on the halfway line. The rules were a bit like volleyball, albeit with the trickier skill of using our heads rather than arms but restricted to the same maximum of three touches before heading the ball over the net into the opposing half.

It is important to have someone close to the net to form an attacking spike. Needless to say, things didn't always go to plan, not least when one of us went careering in the goal net and into the opposing half. Cue more laughter, ear flicks and bum slaps. Good clean fun. It really didn't matter as long as we played football all day.

So what happened between these two gatherings to cause such a momentous shift in attitude? Writ-large, the football academy system.

We all began playing for fun – learning the basics with our parents in the park, on school playgrounds and at local junior clubs. One by one we came onto the radar of professional club academy scouts who shepherded us towards the clubs they represented.

If you don't know how football development works – not least how competitive it is both for the players trying to attain the precious few places available and for the clubs competing for the signatures of the most valuable boys around – it can sound like an unseemly, premature scramble to unearth the rare few rough diamonds who may have the ability to be polished to adorn their first teams and eventually sold for money.

The sifting and weeding usually takes several years to complete as players fall by the wayside with others shipped in to replace them as the funnel gradually narrows. The ethics of this system – radically devised and introduced into English football following the formation of the Premier League in the 1990s – has been the subject of much scrutiny in books like Chris Green's *Every Boy's Dream* and Michael Calvin's *No Hunger in Paradise*, let alone countless articles, broadcast features and academic studies.

I hope this book will add to that canon of work by telling it as it is – or at least how it was for my friends and I as six typical, London and Home Counties academy players and also for my older brother Matt, as each of us strived to jump through the varying required hoops at every level, some of us falling, others staying the course.

Sadly, as yet, none of us has reached the elusive promised land of playing the Premier League.

This is *our* collective story, *our* experiences, *our* relationships, *our* thoughts and *our* feelings as we are at the time of writing (spring 2022), narrated and told specifically through my eyes as the author of our combined recollections.

If you don't understand the way the game works (and, frankly, why should you?) it may sound fantastical. You might wonder why and how such incredibly young boys are placed alongside and often pitted against one another, supposedly as teammates but often in stiff competition for the rare few places available at some of the world's biggest football clubs.

So let me tell you about the people you'll read about in this book.

For starters, I've mainly used nicknames to keep things simple. Their real names and brief biographies are listed at the back of this book. I have attempted to accurately convey our feelings, memories and emotions from the time, rather than cold rigid facts.

I have also tried, where possible, (not always easy in football which, above all else, is a game of opinions) to be non-judgmental, not least on coaches and managers who must constantly make tough decisions and balance countless considerations that affected our careers and, of course those of others, which I'm sure were made with honesty, within financial constraints and precious time factors but always without the benefit of hindsight.

That said, at the end of the day, we're also flesh and bone with hearts and minds. Some of the emotions described in this book while not necessarily unique to the lads mentioned, are how we saw things at the time and our own recollections.

When you are young, these feelings can be raw. Situations that mature adults can weigh up with the measured benefit of life experience can send young hearts and minds floating high as a kite or crashing to the ground in an instant. It is easy to get high on the highs and low on lows. It is what life is like for all children and teenagers. Then, as teenage boys, there's all that testosterone flowing around your body. It is a heady mix.

So, to those lads....

Mason was a friend who lived nearby and I spent lots of time playing football with from the age of five competing for our local junior football club (Welwyn Pegasus) where my dad was vice-chairman, and his dad was a team manager. Mason and I had formed a close bond before I joined Watford FC's academy at the age of 10 and Mason signed for Tottenham Hotspur, another top Premier League academy.

Two other boys in our team went on to play academy football - Alex Davey, a notably talented player who was quickly whisked away to a local centre of excellence (I'll explain what this means later) and soon onto Chelsea, where he became a professional player for four years - and Harry Toffolo, who joined Norwich City's academy and is currently a professional player with EFL Championship club, Huddersfield Town - but are not featured in this book.

Beau and Jack became great school mates of mine at Watford, where we developed a close friendship as the club integrated its academy with a local secondary school, a seemingly ingenious, ground-breaking idea at the time as it integrated football training into the school timetable to reduce the need for us to train at night at the end of a school day.

It was called the Harefield Academy and I loved my time there, studying and training hard, and sharing the same experience with my school and teammates for up to ten hours a day.

Spenno joined the school and became a member of our close-knit informal group of friends, having played in the football programme at Harefield even though he wasn't part of Watford's academy.

Lawrence (Loz) was the last to join the group as an academy goalkeeper at Tottenham Hotspur where Mason and I later played.

As a role model we all looked up to my two-year older brother Matt, who joined Norwich City's academy and went on to sign a professional contract.

You might also reasonably ask why I am writing this book now.

After all, most people write an autobiography after they've hung up their boots, whereas I am mid-career – 26 years old at the time of writing and playing for QPR in the Championship (tier two in English club football if you don't understand the pecking order) at a club and with team-mates and a manager with aspirations to return to the promised land of the Premier League – and why not? QPR have been promoted twice (and sadly relegated) in the past decade.

If I am lucky – and it will come down to a mix of fortune and ability as it does for any footballer – I hope to play for at least another 10 years all being well. There are no guarantees, though. A cruel injury, unexplained loss of form, maybe even waning ability or other priorities can get in the way. For now, my aim is to enjoy every remaining second of my career.

You see, I absolutely love football and have cherished the game from the time I first started playing. There are times when I have fallen out of love with it for long periods too but I truly believe those days are in the distant past behind me now and I am back on track. It may be my profession but playing football is more than just a job. It is a passion. I still love training every day and running out to thousands of fans be it a Saturday afternoon or midweek evening.

I have played for my country, well, two actually – for both Northern Ireland and England - in my teens. I have also experienced the thrill of playing in one of the world's best known 'derby' matches, the legendary Auld Firm clash between Rangers and Celtic.

Yet for all the joys of professional football there is a downside that causes pain and anguish. All the lads featured in this book have all experienced good and bad times. I have seen them, and others, suffer at the hands of football and even stop playing football completely as they struggle to come to terms with the ravages it can reap upon the spirit of those who do their darndest to make it. The perception of a footballer's life is often far different to the stark reality.

While most people perceive it to be a constant upward curve of success, fame, fortune, trophies, celebrations, flash cars and money, the reality is usually far different – an emotional rollercoaster and topsy-turvy voyage that for most young players on its downside can include defeat, depression, loneliness, boredom, rejection and, sadly for the majority, failure.

The perks are often materialistic so therefore lack true value and meaning. Although most players will have lots of different groups of teammates in their career, they are unlikely to have few true friends to share their successes with. Don't get me wrong, it is a joy to play football for a living, but you can't ignore the hurt that lots of players or ex-players, like some of my friends featured in this book, feel.

It is for them, and the many thousands of boys who play in academies who don't get to experience the joys of playing at senior professional level, that I have written this book.

More than anything else, it is dedicated to the memory of our good friend Spencer McCall (Spenno) and specifically to raise funds for Sarcoma UK, the bone cancer charity that does such sterling work to raise awareness and funds to support research into this little-known form of cancer.

For obvious reasons, Spencer's story is the saddest part of this book which serves to emphasise that none of us knows what can lurk around the corner or indeed that young talent or character itself doesn't automatically offer immunity to life's tragedies – and yet it is also one that offers hope.

Spencer loved football more than anyone I know and his memory, far from tarnished, is enriched with the joy he derived from playing the game we all love so much.

From Winning Teams to Broken Dreams

CHAPTER 1

FOR THE LOVE OF THE GAME

From the time I can first remember I wanted to win when playing football. Let me be clear, I don't mean winning at all costs by cheating or fouling but by endeavouring to do my best.

My parents were both qualified PE teachers, so sport was a major part of our lives for my older brother, Matt, younger brother Phil and I - and was always fun but competitive. We constantly strived to improve and develop skills that would enable us to play better – even if it spilt into regular sibling rivalry.

Being two years younger than Matt, our back garden kickabouts were spirited and truth be told usually ended up with me losing. It ingrained a competitive streak many younger siblings have – a steadfast desire to overcome age difference to win which inevitably led to heated exchanges. You want to win to wind your brothers up. Winning gives you bragging rights. Dad would often intervene either to decide who had really won or to issue the occasional lecture.

He had been a semi-professional footballer, so although he'd have had a dig at us, deep down, I think he admired our competitive determination as long as we played fair and square.

You can't become a professional footballer without an innate will to win and I don't believe there is any such thing as a good loser. There are only winners and losers and if you don't try to win then what's the point of taking part?

I get that people say the fun is in taking part – but you don't go into a classroom with the same lame attitude towards schoolwork and accepting failure as standard. Sport is fun but also about testing yourself, doing your best and that is driven by a will to win.

All this trailed behind the value of being a good person which mattered most to both of our parents and was passed on to us kids. Mum is a strong Catholic, so we were brought up to go to church and attend Catholic schools. We were taught right from wrong, to accept responsibility and to respect others, respect ourselves and always treat others as you would wish to be treated yourself. I have always tried to maintain these values.

My first memories of football are longingly watching the older boys across the school playground and wanting to join in. In fact, I'd watch and wait for the ball to be kicked over to our side of the playground just so I could kick it back.

Like most kids, l first played proper football for my local junior club – Welwyn Pegasus – when I was five. My first actual memory of the club was watching Matt play in a tournament. His team drew in the final and the match went to penalties. For some reason Matt went in goal and I remember him diving to save a penalty and stop another with his head. From then on, I was hooked and desperate to play, too.

The back garden practice gave me a head start when I began playing for the Pegasus under-sevens team. The first drill we ever did was kick ups which I had been doing at home for ages. While others struggled, I was able to do 10 easily with my right foot and a few with my weaker left foot. The sheer excitement of playing a game at that age was intoxicating. We all looked forward to the weekend with so much excitement. These were special times – literally the best times of our lives before football became more serious. If only we'd known it at the time?

At that age, you tend to enthusiastically chase the ball with all 10 players together around the pitch. It was fun and all about dribbling the ball until you lost it or managed a shot on goal. I recall having to run over to my dad so he could tie my boot laces when they came undone as my hands were too cold. Gradually we learned to space out, pass to one another and play in defined roles. Come rain or shine it was about the love of the game and nothing dampened the excitement I felt each Saturday morning. I get a warm glow now just thinking about it.

It was honest endeavour too. We would usually come home mucky, so mum made me wash my boots outside with a hot bucket of soapy water and a brush. I would remove my boots, peel off my socks, and stand on the freezing cold concrete slabs scrubbing away as my feet went numb and there was barely any feeling left in my hands.

I would see the steam rise from the bathroom window where mum had run a warm bath, then strip my clothes off at the door so she could put them straight into the washing machine, and race upstairs for my well-earned bath where I'd lie back and recall every moment of the game – the goals I'd scored and every other enjoyable aspect of the match. I couldn't wait to do it all over again the following week and would often head straight back outside in fresh kit to play two-touch with Matt and Phil in the garden.

When we were called in for dinner, we gulped it down quickly so we could go back outside to play some more and had to be virtually dragged in at night by mum or dad when it got too dark to see.

Mason and I excelled at Welwyn Pegasus. It was an ambitious Hertfordshire community club that provided football for children in our area and often fielded more than one team in each age group from five up to under-18s.

We were coached by keen parents who devoted time to learn how to do it properly by taking qualifications. This was in the early 2000s as part of a long overdue drive by The Football Association to clean up junior football, which had developed a shocking reputation for poor touchline behaviour, often by over-zealous parents who somehow believed copying the worst antics they'd seen in professional football by bawling and shouting at their own kids and the opposition was somehow motivational and socially acceptable. This also spurred the start of the RESPECT campaign, which has made a difference, even if there is still a long way to go.

For decades, anyone could don a tracksuit and rock up anywhere they wished to supposedly coach at any level of the game. My dad, and many other parents at Pegasus, were in the vanguard of another blossoming FA intuitive – becoming an FA Charter Standard club. To gain this elite award, clubs like Pegasus not only needed to recruit or train qualified coaches and have a well-drilled management structure, but also to have appropriate facilities to play matches which, even in my brief time at the club, moved from junior school pitches onto a larger sports field at a local comprehensive school.

In short, it was a good, well-run club, with our families at the beating heart and soul of it. My dad, just like Mason's dad, Dave, and our friend Alex Davey and his dad, Miles, coached us among others.

As a result, our team excelled, and we won most of our matches. Not that this dimmed the passion for other players and teams at our club who weren't quite so good. There was room for everyone and the internal club rule was that with rolling substitutes (basically, players can come on and off as often as the coach wants) all kids got to play at least 50 percent of the time over the course of a season, which enables every child to progress at their own level.

Summer tournaments were the best days of the year when we got the chance to play mini matches all day. We'd all get up early as a family with mum preparing loads of food which we neatly packed into a cool box. Other parents would bring a gazebo and chairs so they could watch and keep things together. It was blissful.

Looking back with Mason, these were some of our happiest times together as football families among fellow parents and friends, waking up excitedly each weekend morning to the day ahead, devouring breakfast, slipping our boots on to literally play football all day. We lived close by but went to different schools so our time together was all about training and matchdays.

As the club had a good reputation, we soon came on the radar of professional club scouts. If you don't know how football works you might be surprised to hear how young some of the biggest clubs come looking for talent.

Alex Davey was the first to be spotted in our team as he stood out in midfield. At under-nines level he was invited to play for Cambridge United, an English Football League (EFL) club, who ran a Centre of Excellence.

Let me explain what this means. Aside from the changes I have mentioned to the grassroots game, English football went through a revolution of many kinds in the 1990s.

Firstly, the Premier League was formed in 1992, fuelled by the advent of Sky Sports and the massive revenue generated by subscription TV at the top end of the game. England's stadia were also overhauled following the recommendations of the Taylor Report after the Hillsborough Stadium disaster of 1989. The FA then set about rebuilding Wembley Stadium as a revamped 'home' of football with plans to develop a new national training hub in Staffordshire which, after many stops and starts, eventually opened as St George's Park in 2012.

Then came a transformation of youth development. In 1997 the FA decided to replace the old-style professional club youth development programmes, which provided training for players from the age of 14 upwards, with academies and centres of excellence, which offered a more rounded and elongated coaching experience to children and teenagers from the age of nine upwards - a controversial step as it crossed into coaching primary school children - an altogether more demanding ask.

Clubs were mandated to employ qualified coaches with tight ratios on the number of players to coaches, have specialist coaches in areas such as goalkeeping and to appoint fully qualified medical support staff. They were limited to a maximum number of hours they could coach children each week, compelled to provide minimum standards of facilities and employ education and welfare officers to look after the players' non-footballing needs.

The initial expectation was for Premier League clubs to operate fully fledged academies, with most English Football League (EFL) clubs opting to run scaled-down, less resource-heavy, Centres of Excellence. Only it didn't quite work out that way. The mobility between the Premier League and the EFL's leading clubs resulted in almost half of the 92 Premier and EFL clubs eventually choosing to run academies. Later these classifications were broken down into four categories when the system was overhauled in the Elite Player Performance Programme (EPPP) of 2011.

The most fundamental change was that, overnight, clubs could sign and train primary school age children, like Alex, from the age of nine - five years younger than before. They had to live within one hour's travel time of the training ground up to the age of 12 and 90 minutes between the ages of 13 and 16, a measure designed to prevent children feeling constantly tired from midweek training and excessive travelling which could have a detrimental effect on their home life and schooling. This too was later scrapped in the EPPP. Make of that what you will.

It is worth me saying that these were only *football* academies. The boys playing in them attended normal schools, they just trained at clubs on midweek evenings and played weekend matches. Gradually though, as you'll hear, they encroached onto the conventional school week, claiming the boys needed extra time to train at the expense of their schoolwork. Hmm.

Not that I understood any of this at the time, of course. All I knew was that one of the lads in our team could no longer play for with us at Pegasus. It seemed such a natural progression and, of course, we all aimed to follow Alex into academy football.

What we didn't understand – how could we as seven-year-olds? – is that to protect their investment, professional clubs prevent children playing for junior clubs, their schools, district teams and even try to dissuade them from playing other sports sometimes. The aim is supposedly to reduce overplaying but, to me, it seems wrong to stop children from playing with their mates from such an early age. That said, playing for a professional club just seemed like the coolest thing ever and there was a deep sense of loss for Mason and me when Alex left.

Football was my entire life, not just at weekends but also at school where in Year Five we organised our own World Cup, a truly ingenious idea devised by my best friend Chris, who set it up with printed fixture lists and team standings.

Sixteen of us played for the 16 competing countries. Each day we drew two countries out of a hat then split into two evenly matched eight-a-side teams. It was brilliant. One day I'd play for Brazil, the next for Spain. I couldn't wait for lunchtime to arrive each day to compete in our very own World Cup. It took three weeks to reach the quarter finals and the tension rose as each game became more competitive. The good thing was no one was excluded. We all knew whatever happened we would all get to play in the World Cup Final, we just didn't know for which countries.

When the final day came, we scoffed our lunches as fast as possible, raced outside through our pretend tunnel and placed our jumpers down for goalposts. It got a bit heated at times, but my team won so we lifted the trophy and all shook hands just like proper professionals. Chris even made a cardboard trophy to make the celebrations seem more real. It was a fantastic feeling to be a World Cup winner at just nine years old!

The following season was my best at Pegasus and my last at Mini Soccer, a seven-a-side game played on a small sized pitch. The following season, I moved up to 11-a-side football on a larger pitch which was more physically demanding.

By now, we had the best team in Hertfordshire for our age. At eight years old I was invited to play at an Ipswich Town development centre with my brother Matt in nearby Harlow. At the time I just thought this was to improve my football and didn't realise it was a potential gateway to Ipswich's academy.

Matt had attended these sessions for a while and even been to Ipswich's training ground to participate in development centre games. He was a really good player, and I would watch him using his skills and try to do the same things the next time I played.

Development centres are designed to prepare players for progression into the main academy. It is also an opportunity for the club to see how boys cope in this more competitive environment while still being able to play for their junior club. Typically, clubs spread these centres in towns across their region to attract a wider array of talent. Remember all this is going on at under-nines level – for children aged six, seven and eight or younger.

There is no other way of putting it, even at such a young age, you are being groomed for life in academy football and being eyed up as a potential commodity professional clubs hope to polish so they can sell and profit from later. Not that children or parents see it that way.

Scouts had mythical status. Everyone heard about them. Rarely did we know who they were or if any were watching us play. We knew it had happened to Alex Davey but had no idea who these fabled scouts were or which clubs they were working for. It was just something people spoke about. At school, there were constant rumours of scouts watching our games or talk of a friend of a friend going on trial to a particular club.

Matt didn't sign for Ipswich but later joined Norwich City's academy when he was 13 years old. Believe it or not, that is quite late to do so. Like their East Anglian rivals, Norwich also had a development centre close to Welwyn.

We found out that Cambridge United's Centre of Excellence folded after the club's first team were relegated from League Two. Fortunately, Alex fell on his feet and was signed by Chelsea, one of the biggest and best clubs in the country with a top-level academy to match their status.

Back at Pegasus, Mason and I sharpened our focus with the aim to follow suit. We continued to play at under-10s level with our team going unbeaten all season. I was the only kid at our school to play for Pegasus. Most played for Lemsford, who we beat 5-1 to effectively wrap up the league. We had a great team. My cousin was our goalie, Mason, being a natural goal scorer, was our main striker and I was in midfield and captain of the team.

I loved wearing that armband. The build up to games was exciting - like Christmas every Saturday. I never enjoyed the game in quite the same way as either an academy or professional player. There was so much more freedom. I could take a few players on and try to score goals. It wasn't about tactics or winning but purely about fun. As a professional your game is so often focused on calming the opposition and doing a job, not being creative or expressive.

We also won our league cup in my most memorable game at the club with the whole pitch bordered with tape for the final and the trophy and medals on show as we walked onto the pitch. It was my first game shot on video and one of my best matches. We won 5-2. I scored two headers and was awarded player of the match. It was a great day for the team and me.

A scout from nearby Watford FC watched the final and following my outstanding performance decided to invite me to a trial at their academy. This was unbelievable. Watford were a Championship (tier two) club so ran a professional club academy.

The trial lasted six weeks consisting of training two nights a week with a match on Sundays. The first session was nerve-racking. I'd never felt so tetchy playing football before – the pressure of trying to secure a contract, I guess. It seemed a massive step up and I worried whether I was good enough. You want to do well so they will sign you and you're conscious of being judged on everything you do. I felt the tension most in matches. At Pegasus, I had played with complete freedom - I just went out to win. Everything was to gain. Nothing to lose. In these trials, I couldn't afford to make mistakes if I wanted them to sign me.

I concentrated on basic passes and touches which I hadn't needed to think about before. Even now, if my confidence is low, I go back to the basics. It is called unconscious capability, like driving a car. When you are learning you need to concentrate hard on everything like checking your mirrors, clutch control, when to press your feet on the accelerator or brakes. Once you pass your test, you stop thinking about it and just drive. I definitely had my football L-plates on during those first few weeks of my trial so played well within my true potential.

Once I gained confidence and settled down, I was able to express myself more. Motivation has never been a problem for me. My determination has usually enabled me to blast through any self-doubts and setbacks in my career. Whenever I have had a challenge to face, I usually find a way to overcome it. Either way, I must have done enough as they asked me to return at the start of the following season for an additional trial period.

In local junior club football, the end of the season is always tournament time. For me, these were great days that consisted of whole days playing football, eating burgers and slurping ice cream with the chance to win a trophy at the end. What's not to like? Every team at our club took part in four separate tournaments and our team won three of the four we played in.

In the final tournament we travelled up to Cambridgeshire to compete against teams we hadn't played before. We won our half of the draw and in the semi-finals played against our B team who had finished runners-up in the other half.

As a team that had gone unbeaten all season with the best players competing for our A team we were confident we would win again but lost our one and only game of the season...to our own B team. We were devastated and some of the boys cried. That was my last game for Pegasus other than an overseas tournament later that summer which offered a fantastic experience. It was also my first brush with the serious side of academy football.

While on trial at Watford, my dad told their under-11s coach that I was due to travel with Pegasus to play in the Dana Cup in Denmark. The coach said if I went, I could forget about playing for Watford. Fortunately, my dad took no notice, so I went with my mates, including Mason, my cousin Michael and big brother Matt to Denmark for an amazing week-long experience.

Matt was playing in the intermediate age level while we were in the junior section. In total the Pegasus contingent amounted to 27 players and roughly the same number of coaches, mums and dads, supporters and helpers. Also joining us for the first time was another local lad, Harry Toffolo, who has gone on to play professionally and to represent England at under 20 level.

The Dana Cup was a large tournament that attracted junior teams from all over the world. We slept in converted classrooms at a local school where we bedded down in sleeping bags on exercise mats. The food was served in massive tents with hundreds of kids in long queues each day for breakfast and dinner with packed lunches provided as some of the games were a bus ride away from the main centre.

None of this mattered as it was football, football and even more football. Everywhere we went we met boys' and girls' teams from different countries. Girls' football hadn't taken off much in England back then but was booming in some European countries so was good quality.

On the first night we assembled in a huge field dressed in national colours for the opening ceremony. This involved marching through the town as residents applauded. I recall standing on top of a hill looking behind me at what seemed mile upon mile of fellow teams. It was a wondrous, colourful sight with flags from different countries.

We played in one of the younger age groups competing in short games with a big squad so we didn't overplay. We did well and reached the final. In the quarter finals, we played a Norwegian team who scored early on but we equalised just before half time and ran away with the game in the second half winning 5-1. I bagged our fifth and final goal and for some reason I still can't explain did a crazy run back to the halfway line and pulled my shorts down and did a moony. What was I thinking? I seriously regretted that move afterwards as my mum punished me in front of everyone. It was outrageous and out of character and I haven't done anything remotely like it since. I guess it was just sheer joy.

In the final, we met a team from Venezuela who seemed much bigger and stronger than us. They scared us and we ended up being well beaten. I was so frustrated I started to cry on the pitch and had to be substituted while I tried to contain my emotions. The disappointment didn't last long or diminish what had been one of the best and most fun weeks of my life. Following a second trial I was offered a contract with Watford FC, so the tournament had been a wonderful way to round off my time at Pegasus.

During my trials in March 2005, Watford survived a relegation battle at the foot of the Division One, now called the Championship. Two years earlier, along with many other clubs, they had been in severe financial difficulties following the collapse of a television deal the EFL had signed with ITV Digital. Fortunes had changed. By the time I signed in September as a 10 year old, Watford were embarking on a season in which they won promotion to the Premier League via the play offs having finished third in the league.

With Watford playing in the Premier League we decided it was a great opportunity to watch our local club play against the best teams in the land so we bought season tickets. Their first home game was against our favourite team, Manchester United, a 'must watch' match which meant so much we curtailed our holiday and changed flights so we could get back for the game. During the match, my dad received a call from a friend who was a coach at the local Norwich development centre to ask if Matt would like to play in a game the following day at Norwich's training ground at Colney. Matt went along and played so well Norwich signed him that week – proof that sometimes the six-week trial and continual assessment aren't the only route to get into an academy!

From now on my football journey would be an entirely different experience. Like all academy players I would get to play against some of the best players of my age in England, be trained by top coaches and travel the country to compete in matches. We all shared the same dream - to become professional footballers including Mason, who soon signed for Tottenham Hotspur.

Something else changed. Even though it is only a registration form, as an academy player once you sign on the dotted line with a professional club, you are contracted to them and, in effect, become their property. There is no money involved – you aren't paid to play and neither do your parents receive any recompense. Equally you can't play anywhere else either. From now on, if any other club wanted to sign me or if I chose to move at the end of a registration period, my new club would have to pay to recruit me. It is called 'compensation', supposedly for the time the club losing the player has invested in your development, but it is a transfer fee in all but name. Not that any 10-year-old or their parents see it that way, of course. The stark reality only becomes clear as you get older. You may still be a child, but you are theirs to own.

Football was no longer a hobby to be played for fun either. I couldn't go down the park for a kickabout with my mates as I did before. That wasn't allowed. Instead, initially at least, twice a week I would make my way around the M25 to attend evening training and travel anywhere in the country on Sundays to play against other academy teams – replicating the sort of schedule of the senior teams at our clubs with our results assessed to the same exacting detail.

For families, having a son, or as in our case two sons, in a professional football academy is a demanding commitment, both in time and money. I was lucky. My mum and dad were able to drive Matt and I to training sessions and matches. Many players are less fortunate and their parents, for no fault of their own, cannot necessarily support their children in the same way.

At this early part of the journey, all things seemed possible. But there was another feeling that troubled me - although, in time, I would find a much greater sense of achievement playing for Watford than I had at Pegasus, I would question whether it was worth the three days' worth of anxiety beforehand.

The serious business of football was about to begin.

CHAPTER 2

SERIOUSLY

F ootball is seen as a dream vocation – the best job in the world.

For my group of mates and I, any thoughts of the trappings the game might offer - money, lifestyle, cars, and the adulation of fans – were for the future. As 10 and 11-year-old boys, playing football as often as possible was all that mattered. It was always about the love of the game - dribbling, passing, tackling, shooting and scoring goals. From the top of my head to the tips of my toes I lived and breathed the game.

When Mason and I set out on our football journeys we couldn't envisage ever wanting to do anything else. As we settled in at our elite professional club academies, we experienced a different approach. Football wasn't about the fun of testing and trying out your skills or even playing to win matches, but about improving, developing and understanding the game. We worked on our weaknesses and improved our strengths. Winning or losing didn't matter so much, the focus was on personal performance and impressing the coaches who oversaw our progress.

In fact, I stopped asking Matt and Mason how their teams got on and whether they had scored or not. All I wanted to know was how well they had played and what their coaches said afterwards. Once you're in an academy, you are part of a sausage machine geared to grinding out potential first team footballers. The joy of winning or the excitement in showing off your skills had little value.

At Pegasus, I loved the build up to a Saturday game so much I often couldn't sleep the night before a game through sheer excitement. At Watford, my sleepless sensations were fear, nerves and anxiety. I would run the game over in my head, worrying about mistakes I might make rather than how well I might play. This pattern dogged my game for many years. I overthought things. Later this would cause untold trouble.

Not everyone is the same, of course. Mason enjoyed his football. He was a calm, dead eyed striker who loved the thrill of scoring which he carried into his academy career with Tottenham. He'd come through a round robin event organised by Spurs in which 400 or so kids were invited to take part and whittled down to a talented handful of boys who were chosen for trials. A carefree person by nature, Mason enjoyed academy football more than I did at that stage.

As an 11-year-old you hope your dreams will come true – but also fear not being good enough to jump through the next hoop in the knowledge that most young players don't make it. Brutal as it sounds, even at that age clubs often know which players have what it takes and those that don't.

But football is a team game. Even the most talented player needs teammates to compete alongside in games so they can flourish. Only a couple of players in, say, a 15-player team squad might be good enough to progress, but they still need 13 others to help the talented two to develop.

Not that club coaches can tell players, who are still children after all, they are only there to make up the numbers. It is also possible some may sneak through as late developers or simply have the dogged determination to gradually improve.

There are so many imponderables - but it is hard to avoid seeing academy football as anything other than a massive trawl for talent. The evolution of professional club academies, which has brushed schools' football aside, requires clubs to field full teams at each group from under-10s to under-21 level. Before academies, most clubs doubled the age groups and recruited fewer players to keep the quality high and to minimise the inevitable heartbreak for those released along the way.

The cost to clubs is minimal as their outlay is easily recouped if they unearth the occasional rare diamond that may be worth millions of pounds in transfer fees down the line. Most of the expense is passed onto parents in the cost of ferrying their kids back and forth to training and matches.

That is why there is so little room for sentiment in youth football. More than 10,000 boys play in professional football academies in England at any one time – yet less than one percent will reach professional level. Even then the average age of players leaving the game is 21 years old. Given these sorry statistics, it is dangerous thinking for any academy player to prioritise football over their education. Yet that is exactly what most do each year in a misguided belief they have a guaranteed future in football.

I was lucky to join Watford at a time when the club introduced a pioneering project that was designed to integrate schoolwork with the academy football programme, which doubled our training time and fitted into a slightly longer school day. It also meant my football friends were my school mates.

The Harefield Academy was big news when it opened in 2008 and attracted lots of media attention. I was one of a few lucky academy players to be featured by *Sky Sports News*, who followed us around for a day and in *The Times* newspaper, which spent hours taking photos in our garden. As a 12-year-old it boosted my ego no end and was my first real exposure to the media. I felt special, but it wasn't about me, it was about the innovative programme.

It was a tough decision for my mum and dad to allow me to go to Harefield. In my first season at Watford, I joined my brother Matt at St Columbus College in St Albans, a single-sex private Catholic school with a strict regime. I worked hard to settle in and was well behaved, if a little cheeky at times. Harefield was different. Moving from a high performing private school to a recently failing state school was a quandary and mum was initially reluctant for me to go.

Yet the Harefield Academy had lots going for it. It was about to receive huge investment and lots of new state-of-the art facilities that would be the envy of most other schools.

Our school days were long, but we were well looked after. Each morning I was picked up by taxi with two other boys and driven to school. Although I wouldn't return home until around 7.30pm, and a 12-hour day for a 12-year-old pupil may sound unduly long, everything education and football-wise was coordinated and done and dusted on one site with no need to go out for evening training. Each day comprised four hours each of schoolwork and football. Compared to the weekly programme Mason had at Spurs, or my brother Matt, who was now in Norwich City's academy, it was a breeze.

They left school early on training days so they could reach evening training for the 6.30pm start time. They either had to eat in the car – hardly the most nutritional way to digest food before playing sport – and sometimes try to do their homework on the way, which usually proved almost impossible.

Mason preferred to nab a siesta while his dad contended with the stressful rush hour traffic. After training he would typically arrive home between 8.30-9pm usually feeling tired, hungry and sweaty with homework still to do for the following morning.

Fortunately, Matt was able to train one night a week in nearby Hatfield with a group of fellow Hertfordshire players in Norwich's academy so would only need to make the two-hour journey up to Norwich once a week, with dad rotating driving duties with other parents. Like Mason, he usually slept for most of the four-hour round journey.

At 13, Mason skipped one day a week at school to attend Tottenham's academy, which by Year 11, his final school year, increased to twice a week. There's also the isolation that comes with this activity. It isn't easy to share your academy experiences with your school mates. It just sounds like boasting so you don't form the same bonds.

Mason was one of a few boys in Tottenham's academy to be offered a four-year deal at 12 to cover the rest of his secondary school years through to the age of 16. Small wonder he prioritised football over his education. Despite the initial pushback from his school to the idea of day release to play football, in effect singling him out for special treatment, they eventually conceded.

Matt also took either one or two days a week off school. This would be a full day away from school spent travelling and to train in Norwich, a four-hour round journey remember, which left little time to catch up with his studies which he had to cram in whenever he had time and resulted in him missing out on time to socialise with friends.

Prioritising football over education was made to seem normal and the sort of sacrifice expected of thousands of boys across the country. Parents barely ask questions or express reservations for fear of it being construed as a sign of negativity which might eventually cause their son to be released. No parent wants to take the dream away from their child. The clubs have complete control and they know it.

By comparison, Watford's programme at Harefield made so much sense, even though, back then, they were the only UK club with the vision to merge school time with academy football. It seemed such obvious logic – increase the training time for academy players who attended the school. Traditionally, academies usually trained for two hours on two or maybe three weekday evenings. Matches always took place on Saturday or Sunday, so each player received approximately five to seven hours coaching plus their game time per week. At Harefield, this increased to 10 to 15 hours a week within the school day.

I absolutely loved it. Not just because I was playing more football but also because Harefield was where I became close school friends with two of my fellow Watford academy teammates, Beau and Jack, and where I met Spenno, who became part of the close-knit circle of friends featured in this book.

Beau and I joined Watford at the same time. I was initially intimidated by him as he was a popular kid with a striking blonde complexion and cool hairstyle. A child model, he was instantly likeable and always up for a good laugh, which is probably why we got on so well.

We shared the same opinion that everyone else at the academy must be miles better than us at football otherwise they wouldn't be there. Daft logic of course as we deserved to be there too. It was only when we attended school together that we became particularly close friends. You might expect a good-looking lad to have a flash of arrogance, but Beau wasn't like that. He was kind and never said a bad word about anyone.

Whereas Beau was a right back, Jack – or Westy as we called him (his family name is Westlake) - and I were midfielders. Jack had been at the academy from a young age which meant his technical ability was that bit sharper than most of us. Although we gradually caught up, it was obvious he was a comfortable, seemingly more mature footballer who got on with everyone, took training seriously and was one of the best players in the side.

Again, like Beau, it was only when we attended Harefield as pupils and started to spend more time together that I really understood the funny character that Westy was, and his ability to make us all laugh. In football parlance he was a low maintenance player for our coaches. Jack led and could take a game by the scruff of the neck from midfield.

Spenno's situation was slightly different. He was an ordinary school pupil at Harefield who had just returned from living in Spain and was a huge Watford fan. A naturally attacking midfielder, he had talent but wasn't part of Watford's academy. Nonetheless he passed an informal trial which allowed him to participate in the school's football programme and we hoped he might become a fully-fledged academy player at a later stage. We bonded with Spenno properly on a Year Nine geography trip and eventually Beau, Jack, Spenno and I became our own mini gang of four.

As the first junior football intake at Harefield, we were also darlings of the school and known colloquially as the Watfords, privileged 12 and 13-year-olds living the dream, improving as footballers due to the amount of training time available and the quality of coaching we received. We were given free school lunches and treated as the most important pupils as our football academy transformed the school into a modern academy with enviable facilities.

We took advantage sometimes by messing around and turning up late to lessons by using football as an excuse. Any time we got into trouble we were cautioned rather than given detention. If we missed lessons because of a football commitment, the teachers would go over the previous lesson for one or two of us even though 20-30 students in the class had already done it. We were even allowed to play in the school football team in inter-school competitions so there were only two or three places for the normal school kids.

Looking back, it was unfair for us to be treated this way and hard on the boys who weren't part of the football programme to miss out even if they did benefit from the investment and new facilities Watford FC's programme had brought to the school.

The downside was that Harefield had been a failing school that had been falling apart – from worn carpets to scraped walls and graffiti. The club and the school's sponsors invested huge sums of money in new buildings, but these facilities weren't ready until our second year there. During the conversion, the playground resembled a building site and some of our classes were taught in Portakabins.

The special treatment we received meant we weren't always liked by some of the other schoolkids. After the strict regime at St Columbus, I absolutely loved Harefield as I went from a school that taught Latin to one that offered cookery as an option. It just felt so much more fun. I made great friends and even had a girlfriend or two.

Importantly, my football improved immeasurably. Our increased training time from five to 12 hours a week meant we stood a better chance of reaching the much vaunted 10,000 hours concept, a calculation thought to be the minimum amount of practice time needed to achieve elite status in any walk of life be it sport, music, art or any other defined skill.

We also had a great group of coaches, many whose careers have progressed remarkably since including current Burnley manager, Sean Dyche, who was our under 18s coach, academy manager Mark Warburton, who is now my manager at QPR and has managed Glasgow Rangers and Brentford, and Nick Cox, our assistant academy manager, now academy operations manager at Manchester United. Aidy Boothroyd, Watford's first team manager when Harefield opened, later became England under 21 manager for five years.

Critics of the Harefield Academy and Watford FC partnership point to the difficulty in separating school from football. The toughest question was what would happen to those boys who are released from the academy but are still attending the school – how would they feel looking on at what might have been? These were problems for down the line but back then our first year at Harefield was deemed to be a high-profile success.

When the new school buildings opened at the start of the 2009-10 school year everyone was astounded. The atrium resembled a shopping mall more than a school and was equipped with the best technology. Standards lifted immediately. As players, we had to be more disciplined. If we misbehaved or were late for lessons, we were punished by missing football sessions.

The football facilities boasted a new gym, indoor hall, Astroturf dome and two new outdoor grass pitches. We were spoilt in having these facilities to use every day which, coupled with our top-quality coaching, gave us the best possible chance of progressing from the academy to the Watford senior team.

Things went so well the club asked my dad to take up the role of business academy manager, which seemed a good fit given his experience of managing businesses and interest in education and sport. He had built up his own business which he had recently sold so it was an ideal fresh challenge. As you can imagine, like any schoolkid whose parent worked at the school, I had mixed feelings. I didn't want anyone to think I might receive favourable treatment.

The pressure was there, though. Our short-term goal was always focused on securing a two-year contract for ages of 14-15, which was needed to reach the all-important stage - whether the club would offer us a 16-18-year-old scholarship and a pathway to a professional contract.

Just as everything looked rosy, Watford's circumstances changed as a dark cloud loomed on the horizon.

CHAPTER 3

UNDER PRESSURE

I n 2009 Watford fell into financial difficulty again.

The club's shares were removed from the stock market and the first team struggled at the wrong end of the Championship having been relegated from the Premier League the previous season.

Following a wrangle between shareholders, a new management team came in with Graham Simpson replaced by Jimmy Russo as chairman, who deemed it necessary to drive down costs and focus on the first team rather than long-term player development.

This was the harsh reality of the football business. Harefield seemed a perfect academy solution for a club like Watford. Recruiting local players matched their image as a community club and an appealing alternative to constantly trying to buy success by recruiting experienced first team players that cost multi millions of pounds in transfer fees and millions more in wages.

It was a long-term vision but the club's more pressing need was to minimise outgoings. The option to divert funds from the academy to the first team cast a cloud over Harefield.

As a 14 or 15-year-old, I didn't realise how it might affect me because I was still playing and training every day so it didn't appear to affect my long term chances of becoming a professional footballer.

Our parents weren't quite so happy. Most of the players were only at Harefield because of Watford's investment in the academy. If the club withdrew from the project, we would be left stranded both in our education and football. After much debate and some cogent viewpoints forwarded by our parents in favour of keeping the Harefield Academy going, the club decided to continue with the school project but in greatly reduced circumstances.

Everything was scaled back. Several staff lost their jobs including my dad. We no longer received free lunches, didn't train in club kit anymore and some of our coaches left, leaving fewer of them to deliver our training.

The taxis that took us to school every day changed too. Initially I had been on a route with two other lads but after the cutbacks we were transferred to checkpoints and journeyed to school via minibus, which took longer and had so many pick-ups we were often late for school.

The cutbacks affected our coach to player ratios, too. We had trained in our individual age groups or split into other groups for positional training. After the cutbacks, we were divided into two larger age groups, which often meant there would be 20 or more players to a session resulting in fewer touches and less individualised coaching. Sometimes in mixed matches 11-year-olds played against 15-year-olds.

As a mature 26-year-old player now, it is easier to see cutbacks as a footballing fact of life. Back then, it wasn't what we expected as a 14 or 15-year-old aspiring footballers. Our training became repetitive and less exciting. Lack of motivation could easily have turned to negativity and despondency as standards slipped. If someone missed a session or was late for training, others would follow suit. We fell into mediocrity and accepted the promising project we had experienced for the past two brilliant years had gone. I began to look forward to my drama classes as much as I did my football training.

It was frustrating as we had been ahead of the game. The volume of training we'd squeezed into our first two years at Harefield and focus on technical sessions meant we had improved at a rapid rate. We had probably condensed four years' worth of training into those two years. A small personal sign was how my weaker left foot became nearly as good as my right. Small indicators of progress maybe, but crucial in terms of our football development.

Harefield was designed to make us better people and role model pupils. It changed from being a football academy within a school, to a school where you could play football. Year 10 was my fourth year in the academy and third year at the school. As under 15s the days of laughing in training were long gone. Our latest club reviews implied Beau, Jack, and I were on track to be offered scholarships at the age of 16, even though the decision was 18 months away.

There was a more serious approach to training and matches and our squad was pared back to become leaner and stronger. We were maturing physically but pressure on young shoulders can affect your ability to play freely and the fear of failure replaced fun. The pressure was so intense I spent almost every waking minute thinking about football.

You need mental strength to cope in football. As we saw it, if we weren't offered a scholarship we had failed. We'd have let our parents down and wasted the club's investment in us. Unlike exams, which provide provable results, the opinion of coaches would decide our fate. A poor performance felt like the end of the world. A great game made you feel on top of it.

Teenage years are a rollercoaster of emotions enough without such constant highs and lows. As a Man Utd fan from a young age, I often daydreamed in class about making my debut at Old Trafford but shared a fear of being released and hurled ònto football's teenager scrapheap.

We weren't guaranteed game time anymore, either. Up to under 15 level, we'd all played the same number of minutes in each game to help our development. Game time reflected your form and how well you'd trained. Some players only played in the final 15 minutes of matches for months on end creating an inevitable split among boys in the programme. Some lads improved as others fell back and lost their confidence as the dream of a scholarship dwindled. The signs were ominous. You weren't going to get a scholarship from the subs bench.

Among our group of friends, Jack seemed the most likely to win a scholarship. He had been at the academy since he was six years old and was a consistent, strong, versatile player who was good with both feet. He had confidence so dominated matches from the centre of the pitch and never pulled out of a challenge. He started the under 15s season playing most matches in the year group above - confirmation of his progress and reward for his dedication. He deserved the opportunity to challenge himself at a higher level to accelerate his development.

A few other players in our age group had also stepped up. Much as Beau and I tried hard to join them and although we never quite made it our effort earned us more game time. The hard work I had put in over the past few years seemed to be coming to fruition. It wasn't quite the same for Beau, whose biggest let down came at the most prestigious of youth tournaments.

Just before the start of that vital under 15s season, we competed in the esteemed Milk Cup in Northern Ireland – a highly rated three-tier tournament, which began in 1983 and is now called the SuperCupNI with the finals shown live on TV and games played in stadiums across the province.

Some of the biggest clubs and future stars in world football have played in the competition including Barcelona, Manchester United, Manchester City, Liverpool, Rangers and Feyenoord at Junior (under 15), Premier (under 17) and Elite (under 21) levels. This upper tier has traditionally attracted teams beyond Europe including Brazil, Mexico and the USA. Manchester United's so-called Class of '92 - David Beckham, the Neville brothers, Paul Scholes, Nick Butt and co - all played in the Milk Cup, so too did Ryan Giggs, Wayne Rooney, Gareth Bale, Harry Kane, Sergio Busquets, Falcao and Mats Hummels among others.

In short, the Milk Cup is a big deal in youth football. My first opportunity to go had been as a 12-year-old the previous season with our under 15s team (our 1993 year group). I didn't get to play as I went mainly for the experience. The following summer was different. Although many of my age group players were still a year younger than many others taking part, some of our team including myself, Beau and Jack, went in the hope of competing in lots of matches.

It was the first time I felt like a proper footballer with local people attending the opening ceremony and kids asking for our autographs. We reached the final which was a massive achievement for a small club like Watford and was played in front of thousands of fans at Coleraine FC, where the opening ceremony had been held.

We had a great team spirit with bags of confidence and belief among our team. Our opponents, Everton, also had some very good players and were favourites. I recall feeling nervous as we played *I've Got a Feeling* by The Black Eyes Peas in our dressing room, just as we'd done before our other games. Tonight's going to be a good night, as the lyrics say.

Sadly, it wasn't. We lost 4-1 to a stronger, more experienced Everton team. It didn't diminish our sense of achievement though. The whole week had been amazing. We played matches every day in a festival format that was so different to our normal academy programme. There are lots more tournaments in academy football now which is good to see and, in my opinion, is something that should be fostered from a young age.

Jack and I played in most matches so felt on top of the world. However, Beau played just 10 minutes across the six games. At the end of a demoralising week, he burst into tears and when he asked our team manager why he had been sidelined he was told he'd be better suited to the following year when our age group would be the oldest in the under 15s category.

This made sense and all year Beau was buzzing about playing in the tournament in the belief this would be his year to shine. Yet when the first game came, to our surprise, a younger player started in Beau's place. In fact, he didn't play a single minute so the whole tournament hammered his confidence and he was left feeling shattered and embarrassed. Worse still, with the cutbacks we'd had to pay our own way to get there.

I couldn't believe it. I thought Beau had had a good season and was progressing well, but the writing was now on the wall going into our final school year. His place had gone to a younger boy. I saw my best mate suffer and while I appreciate it must be a difficult balance for coaches to keep everyone feeling fully motivated and positive, how Beau was treated opened my eyes to the harsh realities of football. Football was never quite the same for me after that.

I had mixed emotions. I was playing well while my best mate was suffering. Don't get me wrong, I don't want to be hard on our coaches. They said nice things when they pulled you aside to let you know how well you were doing or how you could do better. If they got frustrated it was because they were passionate and cared so much. When the money was cut and it looked unlikely we could go to the Milk Cup, our coaches, led by Nick Cox, realising how desperate we were to go to the tournament, devised fundraising ideas including bag packing at Tesco in Watford.

Despite my feelings about Beau, I really started to build my own confidence. I had been selected for Watford's under 15s when I was 13 and stopped being pushed from one position to another. I found consistency in the middle of the park and had gone from being average to one of the better players in our team.

The best weekend of my career at that time came when I played an away Saturday game at Southampton two years above my age group. I thought I was going to make up the numbers but was thrown on with 20 minutes left. We got battered and lost 6-1 but I played well and our coach, Nick Cox, was full of praise afterwards. This felt special because I hadn't just moved up two age groups and held my own but shown glimpses of real quality. It gave me loads of confidence.

The following day we played a local derby game against Arsenal in my own age group. These were always special matches as they had some of the best players around in youth football which meant we rarely beat them. Buoyed by my experience from the previous day, I was more excited than nervous – a feeling I hadn't experienced since my days at Pegasus and had my best game since I'd joined the academy, scoring a hat trick in a 4-0 win to complete my best weekend in football to that point. It sent ridiculously positive thoughts running around my head. I felt certain I was going to be offered a scholarship based on what I had just done.

In football you must guard against such over-confidence as it can easily lead to arrogance. You can start trying to do things you wouldn't usually attempt and if it comes off, fine, you wonder how you did it, but when you make a bad pass or have a poor spell in a game it can have a detrimental effect. Suddenly you don't want the ball. Your body stiffens and you just want to get off the pitch as soon as possible. Imagine this at 14 years old? A football-mad boy in love with football but doesn't want to play? That was me so many times. All the lads featured in this book felt this way at one time or another – the fear of failure and a lack of self-confidence. The enjoyment gone. No-one mentioned it at the time, of course. You internalise it to avoid seeming weak – but it is there all right. You learn to live with it.

At that age you also lack the maturity to handle the rollercoaster so tend to suffer in silence. The problems are worse for kids who replay things repeatedly over in their heads. That was me. If I was put on the left wing, I worried if it was because they preferred other midfielders in the centre of the park. Each time I was substituted, I'd agonise over whether it was because I hadn't played well enough or was, as mentioned, a tactical change. I wish at times I hadn't had such a lively mind. There is a danger with so much at stake to get wound up by every decision. After a great weekend, I'd sometimes feel I'd nudged nearer to accomplishing my next target – getting that all important scholarship even though it was still a year away and so much could yet still happen.

My good form led to me being selected to play for Northern Ireland – the country of my mum's birth. Although I didn't *feel* Irish, it meant I was as much Irish as I was English.

My debut came in the Victory Shield, an under 16s home international tournament held between England, Scotland, Wales and Northern Ireland that began in the post war era at under 15s level until 2001 when it moved up to an under 16s competition in line with UEFA rules. In 2015, England pulled out to be replaced by the Republic of Ireland.

It was another chance to be seen on TV with our first game against Wales played at Port Talbot. After my dad dropped me off at the hotel we spent the next few days preparing for the game and I did my best to settle in among my new teammates.

Most of the lads knew one other having played together in Ireland for years. As the only English-based player in the squad none of them knew me so I felt a bit of an outsider. This was a big step up and I was so nervous in the build up to the game my body froze completely in the changing room. Although I had been gutted to be named as a substitute, I still had to take my place in the pre-match line up on the pitch as the national anthems were played. Nerves turned to embarrassment as, positioned at the end of the row, the TV camera fixed on me as the national anthems began. I hadn't considered learning the words to *God Save the Queen* and hadn't planned to sing along but when the camera came close and focused on my face for 30 seconds I panicked and attempted to sing. After what seemed like an age, the camera moved along the line, but I was sure I had already humiliated myself.

I didn't get to play in the game. Afterwards our coach, Dessie Currie, messaged my dad to say he thought I looked too nervous to take part. This is understandable for any young player going into a strange environment, so I didn't beat myself up for feeling out of my comfort zone. It was all part of the learning curve and a gentle start to my international career. Despite the distractions at Harefield and nerves in joining the Northern Ireland Victory Shield squad, my under 15s season had been a good one and I went into the summer break with lots to look forward to. Potentially this was to be my last long summer break as there was a good chance the following year, all being well, I would begin training on July 1 with Watford's professional players at the start of my scholarship.

A big year lay ahead. For most children, their final school year is focused on their GCSEs which shapes their academic and career futures. Academy footballers have that to contend with too, but the main aim is to prove you are good enough to become a full-time footballer as a 16-18-year-old scholar. It is make or break. Football wasn't a relief from revision for exams. It was where we were truly tested.

Matt was also a Northern Ireland international by this stage and had been selected to play for the under 17s team and, later, at under 19s level. He was in the first year of his scholarship at this point – something I aimed to emulate of course – and had moved to Norwich and was living with a local family.

Despite joining the academy at a later stage than most he was one of the earliest to be offered a scholarship. Although his football went well, he found the first few months hard going, a combination of being away from family and friends and getting used to full-time training. Matt also lived in a small village near to Norwich's training ground that had one daily bus into the city centre so there was literally nothing to do after training each day. All he could do after training was go back to his digs and stay in his room.

At the start of his second season, one Sunday at the end of summer and having seen his friends return to school, he went back to Norwich but couldn't stop crying. It was a feeling of loneliness and isolation.

CHAPTER 4

DECISIONS, DECISIONS

U nder 16s really is the year of decision in academy football.

Our squad was made up of 16 players including a goalkeeper, six defenders, four midfielders and five attackers. We knew Watford would only offer scholarships to, at most, half of us. No matter how much your fellow team-mates were your friends, they were now your rivals.

One decision was already made. Our main striker, Bernard Mensah, was attracting interest from top Premier League clubs. Strong, powerful and fast, he was that precious football commodity, a good goal-scorer. Like the rest of us, Bernard was tied to Watford for the season but at 16 he'd be free to join another academy – albeit Watford could claim compensation for the time spent developing him.

This is a transfer fee in all but name, and while players frequently move from one club to another for all kinds of reasons, it is there to protect smaller academies being constantly raided by larger clubs who can use their financial muscle and pulling power to obtain the best youth players and avoid paying transfer fees for professional players down the line.

Bernard was well ahead of the rest of us. He looked the complete striker so was offered a scholarship and promoted to the under 18s youth team at 15. That left 15 of us to fight for the remaining scholarships.

A scholarship is a two-year football apprenticeship blending full time football training with vocational further education. At the end of your scholarship, players are either offered a professional contract or released. That was for the future. The here and now for us was to fight to win a scholarship -- the next hoop we had to jump through.

We still had to do well in training but were now told our performances in matches would determine our destiny. Our coaches delivered a presentation to players and parents to explain how the decision would be made -- the criteria we'd be judged by, when they would let us know, how each player would be told and our potential options afterwards.

We were also categorised into a three-tier grading system consisting of three ability groups, A, B and C. Obviously, we all wanted to be A grade players and if you were in that group, you seemed nailed on to be offered a contract. Those in the B category stood an even money chance. If you were category C, the odds seemed stacked against winning a scholarship. We all left motivated and determined to be category A grade players, the message ringing loud in our ears – matches mattered most.

Jack, Beau and I were best friends and teammates but now they were my competition. That's why football is so uniquely ruthless. When you sit exams, you don't do so to someone else's detriment, you're doing it to pass and get the best grade possible. Football academies are different. We stood in each other's way. It was specific with Jack as we were both midfielders.

Beau had his competition, too. He'd been signed as an agile defender, a good technical player who read the game well. As explained, his confidence had gradually waned. At 14, Watford recruited defenders who were physically bigger than Beau, who was always the smallest player in our team. He'd spent much of the previous season on the bench and had endured that demoralising Milk Cup experience in the summer. Now 15, he needed to show what he could do. His coaches continued to praise him and offered information that implied Beau might still be on track for a scholarship even though the rest of us could see the tell-tale signs.

It was less now about teamwork and more about on field decision making so you looked better on the pitch than others. Matches matter most, remember, so you start making choices to forward your career rather than what is best for the team. If I picked up the ball in midfield, say, the temptation was to open things up and get a shot on goal. A 'worldie' would get you noticed and stay in the memory bank longer than a sensible square pass to a team-mate.

It seems ridiculous looking back. It just wasn't confined to Jack, Beau, and I. Spenno was also at our school hoping against hope to come onto Watford's late radar for a scholarship, unlikely though it seemed, and Mason waited on similar news from Spurs.

Up at Norwich, Matt was now thriving as a second-year scholar, playing in every youth team game, accepting more responsibility, growing in confidence and getting accustomed to the life of a full-time professional player.

As for Spenno, although he had always trained with Jack, Beau and I, he wasn't actually registered to the club's academy so opted to play for Wingate & Finchley under 16s every weekend. They were a non-League club so lacked the same facilities as professional club academies but could still provide a pathway into senior football.

Designed for players who weren't maybe quite good enough to attain a scholarship, via a college programme that balanced further education with football training, Wingate & Finchley could offer a further education route into semi-professional football at a decent standard. Students would most likely study a BTEC in sport and train a few days a week with a weekly games schedule.

Spenno expected to follow this path after leaving school – a similar step taken by Lawrence, who was yet to be welcomed into our group and who you will read about later in this book. Having been released by Brentford and unable to find a professional club, Lawrence eventually attended a local college programme run by Tottenham Hotspur. Watford also offered a sixth form option football programme at Harefield.

Each time we met the conversation was dominated by thoughts on the scholarship decisions that would determine our future. What Jack, Beau and I didn't expect was for those evaluations to be revealed at our mid-season review.

Watford, like all academies, provided two reviews each year – one before Christmas, another at the end of the season in May. The aim of this continual assessment is to ensure there are no surprises when important decisions are made such as a player being released or retained.

Reviews were attended by the player and one of his parents, the academy manager, assistant academy manager and your specific age group coach, and were held at the club stadium rather than at Harefield. This seemed perfectly normal as dad and I drove the 30 minutes or so from home to Watford's Vicarage Road ground for my final mid-season review. We hoped to hear I was on track for that important final decision to be made sometime in the new year.

Yet when we parked up, we met Beau and DeReece, another player from the team, who had just been told he was being released. My body stiffened instantly, and my mind went blank. I felt terrible for him and didn't know what to say. DeReece was with his mum and grandad, who always watched every game, and was visibly upset. As influential player who rarely a missed a match, we thought he was a definite for a scholarship. As we chatted to DeReece, I spotted Beau and his mum going into their meeting.

DeReece had nudged a place in our team at Beau's expense. If he wasn't offered a contract, Beau stood no chance and surely knew this by now. He felt terrible going into that meeting.

As we said our goodbyes to DeReece, his grandad assured me I would be fine. I wasn't so sure. DeReece was a 'definite' in our eyes. What chance did I stand? My concern switched back to Beau. I sat there with dad for what felt like an eternity hoping against hope that Beau would emerge with a smile on his face. I saw straight away it wasn't. What can you say in these instances? We were 15-year-old mates who had been through so much together. I gave him a hug and told him everything would be okay. He put on a brave face but I knew Beau would cry his eyes out on that car journey home. So near and yet so far.

Now it was my turn. Dad and I were met by Nick Cox who guided us into a room with fellow coaches Barry Quin and Dave Reddington. My heart pounded and my hands were sweaty as they opened the meeting by announcing their decision. I wasn't being offered a scholarship and they explained their decision for another 10 to 15 minutes. I was numb and unable to digest anything they said so just stared straight through them, unresponsive. Dad answered their questions as he knew if I tried to speak, I'd probably burst into tears.

As the meeting closed, they offered to help me find another club, listing some smaller clubs where they had good contacts. I felt insulted. So that is what you think of me? A lower league player. Having been released, they were now telling me what level they thought I could play at.

Dad jumped in and told them we would sort it out ourselves. Neither of us said a word as we walked back to the car in the chill evening air. We just sat there in silence. The news broke me in two. All that hard work for all those years hadn't been good enough.

Dad, thankfully, slipped into parental mode and did his best to keep my spirits up. Calmly, he told me not to be upset, this wasn't the end of the road. There were loads of other clubs out there. He believed in me which was such a confidence boost. On the journey home something stirred. More than anger, it was positive energy. People always define anger as a bad thing but right now I felt more motivated and determined than ever. I wanted to go home and go straight into the garden to practise. The only thing on my mind was PROVING THEM WRONG.

Unlike Beau and I, Jack was offered a scholarship. We chatted on the phone, and I was pleased for him as he had achieved what he'd worked so hard for and richly deserved it. There was no escaping that Beau and I felt we'd failed. As we discussed other player decisions, we were surprised to discover that three or four other players we thought had been certainties weren't offered contracts and a few we didn't think were good enough got them. The crazy world of football we all thought we knew surprised us all.

That night, I lay in bed staring at the ceiling, trying to work out what I'd done wrong and what I could have done better. I was the only midfielder out of four who wasn't offered a scholarship. What did they have that I didn't? What was I going to do now? These thoughts ran over and over in my mind until I came back to the feeling I had in the car journey home. I was determined to show them how good I was.

First, I had to cope with the next day at school. This was a real downside to the Harefield academy model. Most of Watford's players went to the school so the only topic of conversation the next morning when we met in the canteen as usual for our daily chats before school started was the scholarships.

Just five from the 10 players in our age group who attended Harefield (the other players didn't attend the school) had been offered a scholarship. These were difficult moments. None of us knew what to say to one another. Some lads were staying on as full-time scholars, others were leaving in the hope of finding another club. All of us had to see the school year through – but those of us who hadn't been offered a scholarship had to carry the weight of disappointment on our shoulders. The worst thing was training with coaches who had just told us we weren't getting a deal. I felt embarrassed by everyone's good wishes. I just wanted to go home so I could work out what to do next.

That night I sat down with my dad to talk through our options. There was no point looking backwards. That said, I needed to find out why I hadn't been offered a contract. I hadn't absorbed what the coaches had said the night before as I was so upset, so decided to meet the academy manager the next day to find out why I was being released.

Then we drew up a plan of action. I would attend as many trials at other clubs as possible, with dad using the connections he had made with scouts and coaches. Although these clubs already had their own academy players, some would offer trials to players who had been at other clubs, especially those with a good reputation in youth development and players, like me, who had played international football.

We were confident I would get some trials but also knew I had to make the most of them to earn a contract. We agreed that regardless of how many trials I was offered, I would attend all of them before making a final decision. It was possible, of course, that I might fail to impress any of them and my dream of becoming a professional footballer would end.

My mind at rest, I was in a more positive mood than the nightmare of the evening before and next day at school. Not every child has a dad who is so rational and used to business planning. I truly fear for kids whose parents who lack those skills in this sort of situation.

The following morning, I spoke to one of the senior academy coaches who told me my major downfall had been my positioning on the pitch, which seemed a strange thing to say to a 15-year-old as surely having trained for 15 hours a week over four years that was something they should have noticed and taught me to do properly?

It was the end of a chapter in my life. My first academy experience had enabled me to flourish for five years. Looking back, despite my worries, they were good years in which I made lifelong friends, played in overseas tournaments and improved immeasurably as a footballer. It was time to move on.

Players often offer ridiculous excuses for why they feel they have been released. At the end of the day, football is a game of opinions. Ultimately, it doesn't matter what you think, it is someone else's view of why you were or weren't good enough at the time that counts. I don't want to sound bitter so whenever I'm asked what had happened at Watford, I always say it was because they didn't think I had what it took. All I could do now was try to prove them wrong.

That said, I have issues with how it was handled. Ultimately, I was okay because I had good support from friends and family. Not all kids are from a similar failsafe background. They struggle to cope and we see stories in the media of players whose lives are irreparably damaged by the disappointment of failing to make it as a professional footballer. As a mature 26-year-old at the time of writing this book, I wonder if there isn't a better way to cushion the crushing blow for kids who have given it their all from such a young age.

Don't get me wrong, academy coaches have an unenviable task of releasing young players in a business that is designed to leave no stone unturned. They must deliver bad news as the weaker players are filtered out. I get that. But surely the game must shoulder its pastoral care more thoughtfully, not least as some clubs now recruit players as young as five or six years of age?

They barely have any memories of life before being coached in a professional football academy. It is all they have ever known. Clubs come crashing into the lives of children and their families, massaging egos and destabilising the concept of a 'normal' home life.

The entire family structure, their routines, leisure time, who-does-what-when, bend to the will of the club for the time that boy is in a professional football academy. Some lads aren't from stable two-parent families. They'll have single parents, or their own mum and dad may have split up and have new partners. Some come from challenging backgrounds or from fractured communities where crime is rife and young people feel socially alienated.

It is one thing to shatter those dreams in a handful of words but surely the easing down process needs to be measured so it comes as no surprise if or when that happens. We can't prevent disappointment but, in my opinion, clubs can manage expectations far better.

The rest of my school year was disjointed. Okay, I needed to find another club but also had to study for my forthcoming GCSEs. Despite the focus on football, I always took school seriously. As qualified teachers, my parents instilled the importance of a solid education. I was focused on getting the best grades I could. If I couldn't find another club, I planned to stay in education so needed to push myself as hard in the classroom as I did on the football pitch.

It is fair to say most academy footballers believe they'll make it in the game. With the dream so tantalisingly close, little else matters. They don't think about school, further or higher education or work. This is dangerous thinking given the evidence weighted against a sole focus on football at the expense of a Plan B. No matter how talented you are, there are so many factors that can go right or wrong – not just ability and attitude but also injury. The only certainty is there are no guarantees.

Michael Calvin, author of *No Hunger in Paradise* (Century - 2017), outlined the statistical chances of a young footballer reaching the Premier League to be about 0.012 percent from the age of five. During my time at Watford, Chris Green, who has edited this book for me and is the author of the seminal *Every Boy's Dream (A&C Black - 2009)*, estimated it to be, at best, a one percent chance of a nine-year-old academy player becoming a professional football at any level of the game. One percent. At best. You do the maths.

Yet all the talk among elite academies is always about playing in the Premier League. There is never a suggestion of settling down at a Championship, League One or League Two club. Players have great careers in these leagues too. I have flitted between them for most of my career so far. Yet if you'd have told me that at 15, I'd have felt I'd failed.

At this stage, among our own circle of friends, Jack had been offered a scholarship, but Beau and I hadn't. Spenno, who wasn't in Watford's academy anyway, was training with non-League Wingate & Finchley.

Mason waited on news from Tottenham but was fairly confident he had done enough to be offered a scholarship.

Alex Davey, mentioned earlier in this book and still a good friend, was also offered a contract at Chelsea – which was some achievement.

Lawrence, soon to be mentioned and not yet part of our circle, had been released by Brentford and was struggling to find another club.

Matt was now 18 and learning to drive, which was an important skill to grasp when you live far outside of a city centre as he did. Although he was still playing every game for Norwich's under 18s and competing for Northern Ireland at under 19 level, he had decided to start an extra course available at college as back up and was looking forward to coming back after the summer break to try and earn a pro deal.

CHAPTER 5

A TRAIL OF TRIALS

Trials are part and parcel of most footballer's lives and if you want to make it in the game, you'd better get used to it. This isn't casual work experience or a pressure free internship. No one sifts through an applicant's CV or judges you on the strength of an interview. You must prove your worth where it counts most – on the pitch.

When you are released and told you won't be offered a scholarship not only is it a hammer blow but you can't afford to pussy foot around weighing up your options. Going through the motions will just lead to further failure and greater disappointment.

The first choice is to go on trial in the hope of winning a similar scholarship to the one you've just missed out on. The second option is to join a school or college programme that provides football coaching as part of the curriculum. The third and final option is to give up on the dream, go back to grassroots football and focus on your education or vocation. Sadly, after the disappointment, this is what happens to most boys. Some give up on football and even sport completely, drifting away with broken hearts that are somehow never quite mended.

49

While Beau and Spenno relied on Watford to arrange trials, my dad got busy by quickly phoning around his contacts. A week later he had somehow arranged trials at five clubs in as many weeks. Now I needed to take at least one of those opportunities.

As a trialist you're an outsider coming in to take someone else's place. They know it, you know it and the aim of the game is to prove you are good enough to earn a contract. Hundreds of young players face this make-or-break scenario each year. Most are 15-year-old kids who have just been released from clubs they have probably been at for several years.

It is a terrifying experience to walk into an alien environment to steal someone else's dream. Typically, your future comes down to a single session or few days of training. The sole goal is to win a contract. If that means stepping on someone else's toes, so be it.

The assumed direction of travel if you are released from a Premier League or Championship academy is downwards to a League One or League Two club. Yet football is a game of opinions. How one coach sees you might differ to others. My dad had managed to arrange trials with clubs at the same level I'd been playing at. Trouble is, you're swimming in a large pool of similar players who have been released as the same time. Some 700 players in the under 16 age group are released each year among the 92 Premier and EFL clubs – an average of seven players per club. Yet there simply aren't 700 places available – so most will miss out.

First, I went up the M1 to Leicester City. A good Championship club back then but now among the top teams in the country, my dad secured a trial through the under 18s coach. I already knew a few of the lads there as I had played with them for Northern Ireland but that wasn't enough to stop me shaking as I walked out for training. I didn't start well but soon began to express myself on the ball and quickly developed a rapport among the other players. Coaches value players' opinions and seek signs of approval from them. I earned their respect on that first day and after another good session the following day, dad and I sat down with the coaches in the canteen to discuss my future.

A few minutes later former England manager, Sven Goran Eriksson, then manager of Leicester's first team, walked in. The academy manager had asked him to say hello and shake our hands. I was star-struck but Sven was refreshingly normal. It was a big ego boost for me. No messing around they offered me a scholarship there and then. I couldn't believe it. It was an indescribable feeling of initial excitement followed by a massive sense of relief and a huge weight lifted off my shoulders. My concerns about not getting another club had been allayed.

Dad and I stuck to our plan to attend all five trials before deciding which way we would move. Leicester's academy manager wasn't happy but accepted it, hinting that a professional contract might also be on the table. Maybe it was a ploy to sway us to Leicester City straight away but the self-doubt in my ability had been eradicated and I felt pumped up for the remaining trials. I wanted to smash every single one of them so I could choose the club I wanted.

My next trial was at Queens Park Rangers, who ran a centre of excellence rather than an academy. I wasn't too excited about playing at anything less than an academy, but they were close by and might offer an easier pathway to the first team. I went to an evening session with my age group and trained on an Astroturf pitch which was only half lit. I had been spoilt with the excellent facilities we had at Harefield so this felt like a comedown. The coaches arranged a five-a-side tournament and after my experience at Leicester, I played with confidence and again I was offered a contract on the spot. I was buzzing on the way home but couldn't see myself going back due to the quality of the facilities.

With two offers in the bag, my third trial was at Norwich City where my older brother Matt was now in his second scholarship year and doing well as youth team captain. I looked forward to this trial not least as I had rarely seen Matt since he had moved up there and I liked the idea of us playing at the same club.

I was familiar with Norwich's training ground, which is set in the Norfolk countryside, as I had seen Matt play there many times so as we drove through the gates for my one-day trial I had a good feeling. Matt gave us a brief tour and introduced us to his teammates and coaches. Everyone nicknamed me Bally No 2, which made me feel at home.

My trial consisted of a game between a mix of the under 16s age group and the youth team, including my brother and his teammates. Although there was some joking about me playing against my brother, it was a competitive match with Matt and I taking each other on. After about 20 minutes I noticed the first team manager alongside the academy manager. Afterwards the academy manager confirmed the manager had been encouraged by what he had seen and asked how I felt about playing at the same club as my brother. Norwich already had twins there with Jacob and Josh Murphy, so it was fine for them. I said, if anything, I thought playing alongside Matt would help. It was obviously the right answer as once again I was offered a scholarship on the spot and Norwich understood my desire to complete the remainder of my planned trials before making a final decision.

Three down, two to go. The next would prove to be my biggest challenge so far. While Watford, Leicester City, QPR and Norwich were all well respected clubs, Tottenham Hotspur were big time Premier League royalty, one of the top clubs in the country and their highly rated academy produced high quality, homegrown players.

I was offered a two-week trial over Christmas arranged by Bob Harbour, who had originally scouted me for Watford and was now at Spurs alongside Dean Rastrick, who had been Matt's under 16s coach at Norwich. Bob had also taken Mason to the club – another bonus as far as I was concerned. With three options in the bag, I had nothing to lose by going all out for it.

After Watford, Tottenham's training ground in Chigwell was the closest club to where I lived so I travelled in with Mason who had been at the club since he was 12. I thought having one of my closest mates there might make my first day easier but after being introduced to the lads I was left on my own while Mason received treatment for an injury.

This time I felt more nervous than for my other trials. Spurs had some of the best players in the country in our age group with several having played for England, faces I knew as we'd played against most of them at least twice a season for the past four years.

As I sat in the changing room waiting to go out to train, I felt like curling up into a ball. It was absolutely chucking it down outside and the other lads weren't that welcoming. The session, taken by under 16s manager Bryan Klug who is a highly respected youth coach, was different to my other trials with more focus on technical skill. I found it hard at first, not least as I felt the other players purposely avoided passing the ball to me until I found the courage to shout for it more and show presence by getting stuck into a few tackles.

This only seemed to annoy my opponents who responded as if it was a personal attack. Maybe they felt I didn't have the right to tackle them as I was only a trialist? That didn't matter to me. I wanted to prove I was good enough to become one of them. Having built up some confidence, I went for a 50/50 tackle with one of the stronger players. As we came shoulder to shoulder, I bounced off him and slid some five metres or so along the wet surface with mud down one side of my face and my entire kit drenched. Mason recalls how funny everyone found it which magnified how hard I had been trying. When I got up and saw everyone laughing at me, I suddenly felt small but forced a fake smile to pretend it didn't hurt and to show I was capable of being one of the lads.

The rest of the session went downhill from there. It wasn't a great first day, so I spent the evening worrying that they thought I was too weak. Spurs wasn't the sort of club to waste my time or theirs. I half expected them to tell me not to return so I was pleasantly surprised to receive a text from the coach the following morning with a schedule for the entire week ahead.

I improved with each session but still didn't feel I had stood out. After 10 days of training, Tottenham's under 18s coach, Alex Inglethorpe, told me I had done okay but not enough to earn a scholarship. He offered to extend my trial for an additional two weeks, explaining that to secure a scholarship I needed to be better than the players they had so had to do more in training sessions and matches. This was great motivation because they clearly believed I had what it took, I just had to prove it.

Tottenham felt like the right place for me to be. After that meeting, I felt like a new player. In one of the subsequent sessions, focused on goalscoring, even though it wasn't my forte, every time the ball came to me, I managed to find the top corner whether it was with my right or left foot or outside or instep of my foot. Everything worked.

Crucially, I gained the respect of other players. When we were given responsibility to pick our own teams in training, everyone wanted me to be in their team. I couldn't believe it. This had been the best two weeks of my football career so far but when they wanted me back for another two weeks, I had to tell them I couldn't stay as I had another trial to attend. They needed to make their decision based on what they had seen so far, which culminated in my second match for the club.

I'd scored in the first game and had a stormer in the second, with an assist in a 3-1 win. I couldn't have done any more. Regardless of the club's decision, I knew I could walk away with my head held high. As I met my dad outside the changing rooms, Klug escorted us into a room with Inglethorpe and academy manager

John McDermott, who was a powerful influence and opened the conversation by saying how pleased they were with my progress. Choosing his words carefully he asked why I thought Watford had released me.

He wanted to be sure there were no hidden reasons why Watford had let me go, indicating they wanted to check out if I'd behaved badly or had a poor attitude. A contract was on offer but only after their education and welfare officer had spoken to the headteacher at Harefield. This was enough for me to start celebrating. I had always been a respectful pupil so there was no way the headteacher would jeopardise my chances. I was ecstatic and felt I had earned the greatest achievement in my football career.

There was one final proviso. McDermott warned that Spurs wouldn't wait long for our decision. He respected my desire to fulfil the final trial of the five we had arranged but I would need to let them know my decision as soon as possible.

My final trial was the following week at Ipswich Town. I was absolutely knackered as the trials had come so thick and fast. After so many demanding sessions, no matter how hard I tried, my body wouldn't let me play as well as I had for the past six weeks.

Having been offered scholarships at all four other clubs I was determined to make it five out of five and Ipswich's decision came at the end of a long week's training and immediately after an under 16s game on the Saturday. Playing in central midfield, I started well but faded after 30 minutes. Although I got through the game it wasn't my best match. After showering, my dad and I met the academy manager and youth team coach who, like all other four clubs where I had been on trial, liked what they saw and offered a scholarship there and then.

By this time, Spurs confirmed they were happy with the feedback from my school and offered me a scholarship. A huge sense of fulfilment rushed through my body. It was an emotional time too. I hadn't expected to receive a clean sweep of five offers. Now for my final choice. My heart and head said Spurs, but my older brother Matt had just been offered a professional contract at Norwich. Would it be better to follow in his footsteps?

In fact, Matt was one of only two players to be offered a pro contract by Norwich at the time which was even covered by Sky Sports News and his second-year scholarship couldn't have gone better. He captained the under 18s team, was top goal scorer, trained regularly with the first team and named on the bench at 17-years-old in a Championship game. Off the pitch he had received a Triple Distinction for his college work and been called up to the Northern Ireland under 21s squad for the first time.

As a family, we weighed up my options over Sunday lunch. Dad shared my view that I needed to be at the best club offering the best coaching in the best facilities and the opportunity to improve as a player by training and playing with the best footballers around. That was Tottenham.

Mum's concern was what might happen if my aspiration to become a professional footballer failed. What would I have to fall back on, educationally? This would be the same wherever I went – so it came back to football.

My final decision without regret was Spurs so that's where I headed the following summer after leaving Watford, whose decision to release me didn't seem to make much sense now.

The whole episode had been a blessing in disguise. When you are released from a club you can sulk, fall out of love with the game or wait for things to happen. Alternatively, you can refuse to accept what has happened and work hard to prove people wrong. That's what I did, and I have no regrets. I gave it my all and would now join Jack in enjoying our last few months at school safe in the knowledge that our futures were sorted for the next couple of years. With GCSEs coming up, I could put football to the back of my mind, focus on my revision and enjoy my last two months at school.

During the period I was on trial, Beau and Spenno had waited for Watford to arrange trials elsewhere – Beau at Swansea City, and Spenno at MK Dons and Northampton Town. Both had week-long trials starting with an evening session at nearby Stevenage FC, which sounded like an appealing move as it was just down the road.

It was a culture shock for Beau who, like me, had been spoiled throughout his time at Watford and Harefield Academy, where we had the best equipment and facilities available, cabs to take us to and from school, meals and kit provided.

A League Two club at the time, Stevenage was a much smaller operation and ran a centre of excellence, with sparser facilities than an academy. Beau wasn't impressed so lacked motivation. This is what I mean about mental toughness to make the most of trials. Regardless of how he felt, Beau had to accept this was his immediate future so needed to fight his way out of it.

An offer from Stevenage might provide a platform from which to rebuild – but there was more to it for Beau. He struggled to come to terms with being released and missed the camaraderie of us all playing together. Worse still, he came down with glandular fever during his trials, which made it difficult to train and meant he had to delay taking his GCSEs. With Stevenage unimpressed with Beau, and he felt the same about them, both parties left it there.

By contrast, Spenno did well in his trial so Stevenage invited him to join their youth team on day release training from school to see if he could handle a step up at age group level. But when Spenno told them he was also going on trial at MK Dons, they swiftly withdrew their scholarship offer. Spenno decided a bird in the hand was a safer option so rejected the MK Dons trial and accepted Stevenage's scholarship instead which enabled him to continue his career pathway into professional football for at least another two years.

In the process he had overstepped Beau, who recovered from glandular fever to go on trial at Swansea City with the journey to South Wales his last realistic chance to earn a contract as he had no other trials set up. He felt it went well but sadly Swansea didn't agree and decided against offering him a scholarship.

Clearly timing was an issue. Glandular fever can take months to recover from as it robs you of strength – but there was more to it for Beau. Football is a ruthless business. You need to seize opportunities and, aside from technique, you must be physically and mentally tough. Beau has many endearing attributes but just lacked that killer instinct you need to succeed in football. By contrast, Spenno and I had a more overt will to win. We had a little saying: 'We Never Fail'. Silly, I know, but we often said it to gee one another up, which served us well.

Beau was now able to switch his focus to further education and, in turn, go onto university. Initially, he stayed at Harefield Academy on a BTEC sports programme run by Watford FC, which was a sort of halfway house option. His dream of playing top-flight football might be over but he'd still get the opportunity to play football every day, just not inside the academy system. If he worked hard and did well in either for his college team or for a non-League club, he might be able to re-join the pro game further down the line as many others have done.

Mason received much better news. He was offered a scholarship by Spurs but casually dropped it into conversation like it was no big deal. It was a huge achievement. He had been the top goalscorer in his age group there with the enviable knack of finding the back of the net regardless of how well he performed. It seemed to come naturally to him. It also meant Mason and I would once again become teammates again, just like at Pegasus, but in a top Premier League academy.

Before becoming full-time footballers, we squeezed our first lads' holiday in together – a memorable trip to Cyprus, where my mum and dad have a holiday home and we always went for our summer holidays. Six of us shared an eye-opening night out in Ayia Napa - a culture shock for a group of fairly innocent 15 and 16-year-olds who had never experienced anything like it before. These were nights of pure freedom before we'd need to knuckle down for the hard work ahead.

From Winning Teams to Broken Dreams

CHAPTER 6

A SCHOLARLY LIFE

We started the 2011-12 season as full-time footballers. Not quite professionals but learning our trade. In the first few months of pre-season, I found what this really meant – and it was much tougher than I had envisaged.

Scholarship seems such an old-fashioned word to describe what is in essence a football apprenticeship and far more geared to football than education which, in truth, played a poor second even though we studied for a BTEC in sport every Wednesday morning.

At Watford, hard work had been defined as dedication, professionalism and the effort required to become a 24/7 elite professional athlete - which isn't always practical as we all enjoy a packet of crisps or Saturday night takeaway once in a while.

I read books to understand the qualities it took to become an elite athlete. One book stood out, *Bounce* by Matthew Syed which concludes that people aren't born talented, they become talented due to hard work, learning from failure (inevitable for all of us at some point) and purposeful practice designed to achieve results. Before then, being raised in a Catholic family, I had believed God gave me the talent to play football well. *Bounce* and similar books like it offered a deeper insight into what was required to reach the top.

Each day we were pushed hard by coaches who challenged us and gave us a pep talk if they felt we weren't working hard enough. I've always loved training but back then I began to question if I was strong enough. Each day seemed tiring, both physically and mentally.

You have to adjust to the environment too. Many young people start work as the butt of all jokes whether it is being asked to go for a long weight (wait), to get some tartan paint or find a left-handed screwdriver.

For us, it was being around well-known first-team players. Harry Redknapp was still Tottenham manager in my first year and the Spurs team boasted a host of household names like Ledley King, Kyle Walker, Rafael Van de Vaart, Gareth Bale and Luka Modric. I didn't know how to address these players or if it was appropriate for me to speak to them at all let alone whether I should shake their hand or not. It led to some awkward moments and I worried they might think I was some sort of strange kid constantly wanting to hold their hand.

You also can't help wondering if you will ever be as good as them one day. These thoughts swarmed constantly around my head as I tried to build the technique, physical fitness and mental toughness required for senior football.

I had to get used to living away from home for the first time too, moving into digs with a family near the training ground which I shared with two other players. My room was an attic with such a low ceiling I couldn't stand up straight. I had to slide in and out of bed to avoid banging my head. Sharing with a family meant we couldn't just come and go as we pleased and could only watch TV downstairs during specific times.

Our daily regime was 8am to 6pm most weekdays. We ate breakfast at the training ground before 8.30am to leave the canteen free for the first team players, then did our morning warm-up session by 9.30am, again so the first teamers had an empty gym for their warm-ups.

Between 9.30 and 11am, we cleaned the first team players' boots before doing more stretching, speed, agility and power in preparation for the key part of the day - our 90-minute training session.

Training was overseen by youth team coach Alex Inglethorpe, who made sure each session had a specific purpose. Most of the youth team players had been at Spurs for several years so were good all-round players with specific attributes. Mason and Shaq Coulthirst were good goalscorers, Sam Smith was an outstanding passer, Ruben Lameiras had incredible skill and Kenny McEvoy was a fast dribbler. By contrast, I was a decent utility midfielder searching for an identity I hoped to find under Alex's expert eye.

There was a lot of 1 v 1 competition in which Alex and academy manger, John McDermott, looked to see which players would fight hardest to win – ideal preparation for the steely world of competitive football.

After training, we were assigned jobs around the training ground and ate lunch after the first teamers left the canteen. The food was good quality and highly nutritious. Sports scientists made sure we chose the right balance of foods. If we didn't put sufficient salad or greens on our plates, we'd have to head back down the queue to add some to our meals.

We returned to the gym for football related afternoon resistance training. Each player followed an individual programme. Football has only recently recognised the true value of sports science as the game has evolved from being reliant on traditional (some might say backwards) methods of coaching when diet, nutrition and sports science were warily dismissed, to being more openly analytical and scientifically focused.

We rounded off our days with further routine jobs around the training ground before the dubious delight of a 10-minute ice bath. I would head home with my housemates usually around 5.30pm-6.30pm and squeeze in a short nap before our landlady rang the bell for dinner, which we'd eat with the family before returning to our rooms for the rest of the evening.

That was pretty much a standard working day for my entire first year. Although we had a tube station nearby, we rarely had the energy or inclination to head into London after a long day's training. Each young player is different, of course. Jack and Spenno chose to live at home during their scholarships, while Mason lived in Loughton, also close to the Spurs training ground. My brother Matt lived in a tiny village near Norwich City's training ground which had one daily bus into Norwich and a little pub next door which he was told not to be seen in.

By the midway point in our first season as scholars, we had adapted to the life of full-time footballers and played in club youth teams most weeks.

Mason was having a tougher time though. Having been relatively injury free as an academy schoolboy, he ruptured some ankle ligaments while twisting in training so struggled for fitness. To compound matters, he was diagnosed with a rotated pelvis, which can cause problems for your hips, legs and spine. It left Mason prone to repeated hamstring tears – which dogged his progress throughout his scholarship. Each time he recovered from injury, he'd work hard to get back in the team, score a goal or two, then get injured again, denying him the chance to build any proper momentum.

He needed a back massage and have his ankles taped up just so he could cope with the rigours of a training session. This may sound okay once or twice but ahead of every session it is just depressing for a young player. Rehabilitation takes another toll. You train on your own away from the craic and camaraderie of your teammates. This is tough enough for experienced professionals, but it takes mental strength to recuperate while everyone else is progressing and you can't do anything to prove your worth as the clock ticks against you.

Jack got a few games at Watford here and there, but the competition was high as he adjusted to full time football. Beau was back at school enjoying a less stressful lifestyle away from the academy bubble.

Despite having the near perfect scholarship, Matt strangely struggled to adapt to being a professional player. The main problem was goal setting. Matt had strived to achieve his main goal in life – but once he became a fully-fledged footballer, he didn't know how to take it further.

As a young professional he was well down the pecking order at Norwich, who were now in the Premier League so had the budget available to sign experienced high quality international players in his position. Also, new academy rules introduced under the EPPP (Elite Player Performance Programme), meant second team fixtures were suddenly scrapped in favour of leagues at under 18 and under 23 levels. Matt had outgrown the under 18s age group and the under

23 league hadn't yet been established so he switched between training with the academy and first team.

Having played every weekend for several years, he suddenly found himself without a weekly match to play so filled the time visiting friends at university in Nottingham to relieve the boredom. It was the start of a downward spiral.

So now let's introduce Lawrence. I have mentioned he was playing college football – this was in a development programme run by Tottenham's community programme at St Thomas More Catholic School near White Hart Lane. This isn't a conventional route into professional football but suddenly, mid-season, Lawrence (Loz as we would soon call him) was offered an amazing opportunity.

With both youth team goalkeepers injured, Spurs needed an additional goalkeeper as cover. It was only supposed to last for a week but Loz had character in abundance and made an immediate impression.

Not only was he the loudest trialist I'd ever met, at 6ft 4in was an imposing physical presence and an annoyingly positive, bearded guy who connected with everyone and name-dropped just about anyone he'd ever met in football. Being likeable is always a good start for any triallist and Loz had nothing to lose because no one expected the club to sign him as a professional player.

Now, if you are going to come into a changing room and be loud, you better be able to back it up on the pitch and that's exactly what Loz did. He got better with each session and Tottenham quickly revised their plans and wanted to take a longer look at him. That's how quickly things can change in football. If you seize opportunities when they arise, the rewards can be unbelievable. Loz was also my kind of guy. We clicked as friends immediately and I hoped he would stay in the academy.

As Mason once said there was never a dull moment around Loz, and that proved to be the case – not just at Spurs but as one of our best mates in football.

There was another coincidence. Loz was good mates with Spenno as they had trained together at Stevenage when Loz had been on trial after his release from Brentford. Each day after training they commuted into Kings Cross Station then walked to Euston Station where Spenno would take a train home to Watford while Loz went by underground to Kentish Town, where he lived.

This was the sort of story Beau needed to hear as, in theory at least, he was playing in a similar college football programme to Loz and an opportunity might also come his way if he fought for it. The difference was they had completely different characters. Beau was losing interest in football, while Loz did enough to stay for the rest of the season while Spurs took time to decide whether to offer him a contract or not, which seemed a no brainer to me as, technically, he was the best goalkeeper I had seen in academy football.

The rest of us came to the end of our first season as full-time footballers in good condition with a few highs and lows but no major traumas.

At the end of the season a few of us trooped down to Stamford Bridge to see our former Pegasus teammate Alex Davey compete for Chelsea in the first leg of 2012 FA Youth Cup final against Blackburn Rovers. Chelsea won 4-1, and although they lost the second-leg 1-0 they ran out 4-2 winners overall. An amazing achievement for my old friend.

Before we broke up for summer, Loz received an offer from Spurs — not quite the full professional contract he was hoping for but a third-year scholarship so far better than expected when he was asked to join us temporarily. He was happy to enjoy the ride and see where it took him.

Spenno and I were told if we continued to progress, we too looked likely to be offered professional contracts by the end of the following season by our respective clubs.

Jack and Mason hadn't managed to build the same momentum due to injury, but both knew if they smashed their second season, they too stood a good chance of being offered professional contracts.

Jack found his first-year scholarship a tough one because there was such high competition in midfield. Out of the three midfielders that had received scholarships in our Watford team, the other two players had adjusted better and were getting more opportunities to play. A big season lay ahead for him.

After a brief loan spell at Macclesfield, sadly, my brother Matt was released by Norwich at the end of the season, which came as a relief to him at the time as he wasn't getting the chance to progress his career elsewhere.

Although he felt out of the loop and missed playing with the rest of us, Beau enjoyed sixth form, and had focused hard on his studies and enjoyed playing football with less pressure among a new group of friends.

He had also shot up in height – which was good in one way as he was getting bigger and stronger – but like so many other teenagers he struggled with a growth spurt that eventually saw him rise to being six feet, three inches tall. As teenagers who go through this experience will know, it left him gangly and uncoordinated for a time. 'Bambi on ice' is the often-used phrase for it, of course.

There was another experience Beau had to endure – watching the lads in Watford's academy train in the way we once had, full of heart and ambition to make it as scholars and professional players. That hurt.

The hard season as second-year scholars was about to begin.

CHAPTER 7

MOVING ON UP

N one of us were newbies as we returned to our clubs at the start of the 2012-13 season. We knew what was expected and what we needed to do to secure professional contracts.

Mason, Lawrence and I had the added excitement of experiencing Tottenham's amazing new, state of the art training ground in Enfield to return to. The facilities were incredible and it felt more like pitching up at Disneyland each day than to a football facility.

Mason got more games but was still in and out of the team due to his recurring injury niggles. Not what was needed in the last year of his scholarship. I was playing every game for the Spurs youth team alongside Lawrence who continued to blow everyone away with his technical attributes and buoyant character.

Football is a topsy-turvy career and none of us knew what lurked around the corner as nothing stays the same for long. Elsewhere Jack had also began well at

Watford but the first problem to crop up among our group began with Spenno at Stevenage.

The youth team manager who gave Spenno his opportunity left in the summer. Different coaches have differing ideas and while some players suit a particular coach's style of play, others don't. Unfortunately for Spenno, the incoming youth coach didn't see things the same way as the outgoing one.

His face no longer fitted which was tough to take as he felt he had been one of the better players the previous season. Although he was determined to fight for his place, a big problem loomed for Spenno.

At Watford, Jack suffered the worst of all injuries – a cruciate ligament injury which sidelined him for nine months. You have limited time to impress in the final year of a scholarship so any injury that keeps you out for more than a few weeks is devastating. We were all gutted when we found out. This was the first major injury among our group and a troubling time for Jack. Fortunately, Watford put his mind at rest by offering him a third-year scholarship, in effect another season to earn a professional contract. Peace of mind and something to strive for on the long road to recovery that lay ahead.

As second-year scholars we were given additional responsibility and expected to lead the newly recruited first-year scholars by example. I had been quiet in my first year at Spurs and tried to do my talking on the pitch to earn the respect of the other lads but towards the end of my first year I came out of my shell and was more assertive.

Coaches look for leadership qualities on and off the pitch, people unafraid to dig others out which, in football parlance, means being singled out for under-achieving or not pulling your weight.

In my second year I became a leader in our group. To some, I probably seemed a bit of a posh, privately educated schoolboy who'd had everything on a plate. My mum and dad spoiled my brothers and me. So too had Watford with the Harefield Academy. My upbringing meant I wasn't as streetwise as some of the lads. That said, I'd fought to find a new club after Watford released me, a test of my character and ability which I'd come through with flying colours. Training was more enjoyable as I loved joining in the jokes and changing room pranks.

Occasional conflict is inevitable not least if you came face to face with a fellow player after a bad challenge in training. Our coaches didn't mind seeing us show some passion or aggression occasionally as they are signs of a will to win. One day, though, a gym session got out of hand.

During circuit training, one of the exercises was a single leg squat onto a raised step box. When one of my teammates wasn't looking, I pulled the step-up box away causing him to fall backwards and hit his head. The other lads laughed as it seemed a pretty good joke, but he didn't see it that way. Angry and embarrassed, I thought he was going to hit me when he got up. I'd expected him to take it as the prank intended but having banged his head he was raging. He didn't speak for the rest of the session and the atmosphere in the gym was tense.

After the session as I picked up my phone when I opened my locker, I felt someone smash into my back. I fell into the locker and struggled to breathe for a few seconds. I was winded and my neck whipped backwards in shock. The player I had pranked had thrown a massive dig into the side of my back. I saw red and turned around staring straight into his eyes. As I walked towards him, he backed off. I was possessed with anger and others could see it too.

We moved around the table in the middle of the changing room within touching distance of one another. I grabbed his shoulders with my hands and pulled him towards me and threw my head into his face causing him to stumble then turn away. I came back to my locker, with adrenalin and rage pumping through my body. The other player walked out of the room and went to another changing room to wash the cut on his lip.

I had never been so angry before and hoped to never feel this way again. For a few quick seconds I had lost it and had hurt someone. Okay, it was a prank that went wrong but I wasn't sure it deserved a punch in the back.

The physio heard of our clash and after a dressing down sent us both straight home. Alex Inglethorpe called that night to tell me the club wouldn't tolerate my behaviour and I was suspended from training for two days with the other player receiving the same ban.

We soon made up and our relationship was fine afterwards. We weren't in any real danger of being thrown out of the academy, but we were made clear it couldn't happen again.

Our coach considered withdrawing me from a game against Barcelona in the NextGen Cup the following week at White Hart Lane as punishment. I had worked hard to get into the team so I pretty much begged him not to drop me.

When I returned to training after my suspension things were different. The boys had seen a different side to me and knew I wasn't to be messed with. I tried to earn their respect in many ways but gained more admiration in a few seconds of rage than over several months. I just wished I'd achieved it without headbutting someone. I was lucky to be let off so lightly.

That NextGen game against Barcelona was the highlight of our season. We were drawn to compete against Barcelona, Anderlecht and Wolfsburg in a pan European youth competition for elite clubs that ran between 2011-13 and has been superseded by the UEFA Youth League with matches played with home and away legs.

That Barcelona home game attracted 10,000 fans to White Hart Lane, and although we lost 2-0 it was a fantastic experience. It was also Lawrence's debut for Spurs. We drew at home against Wolfsburg and earned a decent away point at Anderlecht before the return game against Barcelona at Estadi Johan Cruyff, which is adjacent to their training ground and holds 15,000 fans. It turned out to be a magical evening when everything just clicked.

We won 4-1 with Shaq Coulthirst scoring a hat-trick and Alex Pritchard getting our other goal. It was an amazing win and a truly memorable experience – not enough, sadly, to take us forward in the competition but a definite highlight of my season, eclipsed only on a personal level when I scored four goals for Northern Ireland under 19s in our 8-1 win against Moldova in the European Championships.

With things going well, just before Christmas Spurs pushed me up into the reserves with our Barcelona hat-trick hero, Shaq Coulthirst. I had trained with the reserves before, but this was intended to be a permanent move which indicated they were pushing me on towards a professional contract. I didn't make any reserve team appearances that season as they had so many quality players fighting for the same positions, but I was making progress and now training with different groups at reserve and youth team level.

Our academy manager, John McDermott, was one of the best in the business and kept a keen eye on our development. He pushed me yet kept my feet on the ground at the same time. He noted I was a consistent player but said he could tell how my game would go before the game began. To me, I just thought it was obvious that if I started well, I'd have a good game and if I didn't, I'd have a poor one. John thought my view was too fatalistic and spoke to me about pre-match routines and how visualisations might help.

Just as top golfers envisage the outcome of each shot, so footballers have pre-match routines to prepare for the game ahead. I could be incredibly enthusiastic pre-match, which meant I often started games like a bull in a china shop. John thought a calmer approach might help me work my way into games and showed a graph of arousal to illustrate the optimum level required for effective performance, which revealed how being too up for a match in advance added stress and anxiety which could impair how I might play over the whole game. With this, literally, in mind, I felt in a good place and couldn't wait for the rest of my season to unfold.

I admired John's academic approach even if I hadn't felt the BTEC in sport I was studying for was challenging me enough educationally or was sufficient for me to stand out from the crowd on the job market if my football career didn't pan out.

Positionally, in my first year as a scholar I was a defensive midfielder but now moved into defence where I played for most of my time at Spurs.

From Winning Teams to Broken Dreams

CHAPTER 8

EMOTIONAL

C hristmas time for football scholars is the same as for most people, a
seasonal break to enjoy the festivities with family and friends.

If we were to become professional footballers this could be our last mid-season
break as players have to prepare for the always busy Christmas fixture schedule.
We made the most of it with visits to our local nightclub which we'd started
going to over the past couple of months having been introduced to the benefits
of 'privilege' by the head doorman.

We weren't yet Premier League superstars but 'footballers' all the same.
'Privilege' enabled us to gain free entry and VIP wristbands which gave us access
to the best room in the club where we could sit without having to queue at the
bar for drinks.

The demon drink was new to me. I had always been told to steer clear of alcohol
as our coaches warned us it could kill our career before it had begun as it had for
many other players. However, having experienced a first drunken night out that

autumn, I figured the occasional night out of fun wouldn't do any harm. Trouble was, I began going out with one aim in mind – to drink as much as possible.

I had always been able to enjoy myself without drink and seeing the state of my drunken mates didn't make it any more appealing. Everything changed at a friend's 18th birthday party. With things going well in football I decided to give it a try, starting with a Jager Bomb, which was a fashionable drink back then. I necked a few, then moved onto vodka lemonade. An hour later I was lying over a chair unable to move. There was no way I could go home in that state, so I staggered back to a nearby friend's house. Over the next few months, most of my Saturday nights were spent getting drunk at parties or clubs.

At first, it didn't affect my training. If anything, I put more effort in for fear of my stats flagging. But partying became a regular thing and soon took its toll. Sometimes I'd wake up at a mate's house on a Sunday morning. If I had been lucky, I would find a bed. If not, wherever I could lay my drunken head. Footballers need to eat the right food, relax their bodies and, most importantly, rehydrate after a game but my body couldn't recover from the physical combination of a weekend match and a heavy night out.

Sometimes I'd rush a curry down and hardly sleep then feel ten times worse the next day because I lacked the nutrients to repair my muscles with the alcohol slowing the process down. On Sunday, I'd eat junk food to make myself feel better then have an early night because I was so tired. By Monday morning, rather than being up for a start-of-week training session, I had to grit my teeth to survive training and get straight back to bed.

It soon began to show. Two months after having my first drink, Alex Inglethorpe pulled me into his office, handed me a whiteboard marker and asked me to list in order the lads I thought drank the most. I only knew a couple of other lads who drank so I placed them at the top and put myself and Mason in the middle. He then took the pen from me, rubbed out my list and wrote a different list, placing Mason's name and mine at the top.

I chuckled inside but this was no laughing matter. Alex ordered me to sit down. Each one of our team had been asked to write their lists. They had all put me and Mason at the top. 'What a sneaky bunch,' I thought, then realised I just had done the same thing. After drinking for two months, we were considered the team's biggest boozers.

The conversation got serious as Alex talked about his own career. He'd played more than 150 games for six different clubs. He didn't drink as he hadn't wanted anything to get in his way. This made sense but, socially, I had just had the best two months of my life.

Before leaving the meeting, Alex told me that if I continued to drink heavily, I might scrape a one-year pro contract but would probably be released soon afterwards. This hit me hard. I respected Alex as a top coach (he is now academy director at Liverpool FC) and listened to every word he said. Afterwards I told Mason I would never drink again.

It lasted a month. In comparison to many of our friends, who were out maybe two or three times a week, none of the lads featured in this book were big boozers really. We didn't drink midweek and not every weekend. It was just a new experience which we came to us late compared to our friends. It was a sacrifice we felt necessary to become professional footballers. Only a few of our youth team colleagues at Spurs drank and it was only because Mason and I were mates that we were made out to be the drinkers of the team.

My problem was on the few occasions I drank it was often to excess. It is part of my intense personality. When I do something new, I instinctively give it my all, sometimes to the point of obsession. I just can't do things in moderation. I have learned to control it now – but even when I took up golf recently, once I got the bug, I soon found myself playing four or five times a week, which is good exercise but traipsing around a golf course for four hours after training isn't necessarily the best way to recuperate.

Obsession can be a positive thing. I have always been a good trainer, for example. To my mates featured in this book, it is a joke to tell or story to share. Dom's obsession with things. Even writing this book. Only Dom would do this during his playing career.

That said, my parents hadn't spotted problems with my drinking as I would usually stay with friends on Saturday nights out. They were also keen for Matt and I to have a normal teenage social life despite being footballers. It was all part of growing up as my dad would often reason that a drink does no harm.

Foregoing alcohol seems a small sacrifice to focus on a relatively short career that can offer so many rewards – but it is also a conundrum for young players. Drink used to be a big part of the football culture but is largely forbidden territory now. With cameras everywhere, top players can easily find themselves on the front page of the newspapers or going viral on social media. A harmless drink can look like a boozy night out whether they'd had a skinful or just sipped half a lager.

Teetotal sobriety isn't for everyone either. Partying and doing things most young people enjoy – years you may never quite get back and the feel good factor of letting your hair down occasionally – is surely part of growing up?

Balance is the key. Learning to enjoy a night out yet manage your alcohol intake. You can't afford to let alcohol ruin your ability to train or compete in matches. Equally, I wanted some good social times and to make memories I could savour later in life.

Who wants to end their career surrounded by mementoes and medals but no memories? Looking back as a 26-year-old, I have gone weeks with or without drink or going out. My football blossomed when I stayed in but suffered when I partied. I just had a bit more fun along the way.

So at Christmas in our second-year scholarship, the balance was off kilter and needed to be got swiftly back on track as the next few months were to be crunch time. Those late nights took their toll. I couldn't keep up to speed with training among the reserves and my confidence evaporated. I wasn't sharp enough, was unfit and felt nervous. I had taken my foot off the gas when I needed to press the pedal down harder so was dropped back to training with the youth team.

Winning a pro contract was a far bigger deal than gaining a scholarship. This was our dream from when we were children. There are many steps to becoming a regular first team footballer, but none more important than winning that first professional contract.

The statistics against it are astonishing. Five out of every six scholars leave professional football before the age of 21. That meant only two or maybe three of our cohort at Spurs were likely to be offered terms. The signs had looked good. I was one of two players from our year group to progress to the reserves, but now I was back to the youth team on a downward spiral when I needed upward momentum.

Things were even harder for Mason. He had proper reasons to drown his sorrows. His effort went into getting onto the pitch to train or play matches because he was always injured which meant he struggled to cement a place at under 18 level. The daily repetition of needing to warm up carefully and overcome his latest injury just sapped his confidence.

Jack's injury at Watford meant his future was effectively deferred for 12 months as he had been offered a third-year scholarship because of his injury.

For the rest of us it was decision time…again.

Spenno knew his fate early on as he had hardly played for Stevenage so moved on loan back to Wingate & Finchley to get some game time under his belt. As expected, Stevenage didn't offer him a deal. Indeed, only one player in their youth squad was awarded a professional contract.

At Spurs, Lawrence completed his third-year scholarship in style and did enough to earn a one-year professional contract, an amazing achievement for someone who came through a college programme.

Among my age group at Spurs, 16 of us waited anxiously for our decisions and were called into the academy manager's office one by one after training. Mason went in ahead of me. It wasn't good news. He was devastated and his world came crashing down even though deep down he must have known his injury problems had weakened his chances. He just felt numb.

Strange, isn't it? Young, fit, healthy sportsmen reduced to a catatonic state. Just as I had done at Watford, Mason couldn't even look his coaches in the eye as they delivered the sad news. Instead, he just stared to the floor, feeling his world closing in on him. Mason recalls wanting to curl up into a ball and die. I was gutted for him, not just because he was a mate but because injury had prevented him from being able to show what he might really be capable of.

Several other players received the same sad news and the fear of not knowing what might happen next. I waited for what seemed an interminable time for my meeting and when I was eventually called in, I felt better prepared than I had for my scholarship decision at Watford two years earlier even though, like all players, I was on my own rather than alongside my dad. Even so, my palms were sweaty as nerves ran riot through my body.

The coaches were academy manager John McDermott and Chris Ramsey, our reserve team coach. As I sat down, McDermott pulled out a portfolio used to methodically plot each players' performance. On the first page was a circular diagram like spokes on a bicycle wheel to rank different aspects of my game from one to 10.

I scanned it briefly to see how they rated me in specific areas. For example, I was awarded a seven for my ability to run with the ball. My lowest ratings were for heading and my presence in the penalty area. Nice though they were, these diagrams didn't help right now. All I wanted to hear was whether I was going to be given my first professional contract. The answer was mixed. Not a professional contract but a third-year scholarship offer. They still weren't convinced about me and wanted another year to see if I could progress.

My mind went blank. Like Mason, I stared at the floor and try as hard as I might not to cry, I couldn't help it. The news hit me worse than anything in my life. I couldn't breathe and felt a need to get out of the room as fast as possible.

I can't remember their exact reasoning because I was so upset. They felt I needed more time to master the centre back position they had moved me into. I had shown good work but needed to improve important areas of my game.

All I knew was how upset I felt. Not just because I hadn't done enough but how it was handled. At Watford, it came out of the blue. At Spurs, we'd waited interminably so were at our wits' ends by the time our meetings took place. I'm not sure of the best way to manage these meetings, all I know is that neither option I experienced helped in such crushing moments. Looking back, I question whether it could be done in a different way. My honest thoughts are that there should be no shocks or massive surprises.

Mason believes it might help if it was done with less of a fanfare, that it might be better if players were pulled aside and told in their own way on different days. Personally, I'm not convinced there is one perfect fail-safe solution, it just hits you hard regardless.

My mum used to say there wasn't a reason to cry over football. Family and friends falling ill or dying is a cause to cry but not football. Physically, I just couldn't help it. I had worked so hard and couldn't understand why my efforts hadn't merited a professional contract. I didn't even shake hands with the coaches. Not because I was rude but as I just wanted to get out double quick. I rubbed my eyes, went back to the changing room to change into my own gear and got straight into my car.

I cried the whole journey home. Not just a few sniffs either but full wailing, unable to stop. Looking back, I don't know how I was able to drive. The smart move would have been to pull over until I calmed down. I was just desperate to get home and by the time I got there I had just about stopped crying. I flopped on a sofa in the kitchen where my mum and dad came and joined me. Then I burst into tears again. I had given everything. My whole life led to this moment. No other thought had entered my head other than a robust belief that I would win a professional contract. The pathway I had taken and feedback I'd been given pointed that way. Yet I still hadn't done enough.

Mum and dad were as shocked as I was. It took half an hour for me to stop crying and none of us knew what to say. It had meant so much for me to achieve my dream. I felt I had failed. What would I do next? If I went back to Spurs as a trainee, I would now be too old to play youth team football. Great.

I know what many of you will be thinking. Still in there – just not as a professional yet. Further time to impress. Don't knock it, son. If you weren't good enough, they would have drummed you out. Well, yes, and in time I would reflect on this, but at the time my dream looked to be fading fast. It was a bitter pill to swallow.

So what of the other lads featured in this book?

Having been released by Norwich, Matt was offered several trials but chose to join Stevenage FC, as it was closer to home and they had recently been promoted to League One so seemed to be a club on the up. Spenno was also still playing there. Sadly, that first season went badly for Matt. He spent most games on the bench so went on loan to non-League Farnborough to get some games under his belt.

Mason and Spenno both faced an uncertain future. Being at a top Premier League club was surely going to provide Mason with the opportunity to go on trial in the hope of earning a pro contract elsewhere. Spenno, by contrast, had decided to join Wingate & Finchley after his loan spell so got to play in plenty of games. His brief academy journey was over, but his semi-professional career was already underway.

Beau finished his second year in sixth form and was off to study sports science at the University of Hertfordshire in Hatfield, where he could also play football as the university had a good reputation for sport.

Jack and I were in limbo land. We were still technically scholars but weren't yet fully fledged professionals.

As I left the Spurs training ground on the final day of the season, I was gutted not to be returning as a professional footballer. Once again, I had to put the disappointment behind me and come back more determined than ever to prove myself worthy of a pro contract.

I can understand why so many players lose their motivation with so many hoops to jump through and the rollercoaster of emotions involved. I spent the next few weeks wondering if I really wanted to continue. Football had given me some great moments, but also some unexpected lows and I had no idea what was going to happen next.

Flying high at Pegasus. Winning our league cup in my best game for the club got me spotted by Watford. Mason is front row, far right. I am front row, second left.

International adventures at the Dana Cup in Denmark. I am second right on the back row. Mason is to my left. Harry Toffolo is on the front row, far right.

Left: Honing my skills at Watford's academy ©Alan Cozzi. Right: Winning the national schools Under 15s cup with Harefield Academy. Our team included Beau, Westy, Spenno, Bernard Mensah and me.

Left - My first day at work as a 16-year-old Spurs scholar.
Right – My England Under 20s debut versus Romania in 2014. ©Alamy

Feeling like a big name signing – joining Rangers on loan from Spurs at the start of a memorable season.
©Willie Vass

Lifting the Petrofac Cup - one of two trophies I won with Rangers. ©Willie Vass

Spenno celebrating – this book is dedicated to our much loved friend.

Beach boys. Our first mates' holiday before becoming full time footballers. Back: Me, Mason, my friend Harry Butrimas-Gair. Front: Westy, Alex Davey, Michael (my cousin), Beau & Spenno.

CHAPTER 9

LIFE AMONG THE PROFESSIONALS

I weighed up my options over the summer months of 2014.

If I gave up my dream of trying to become a professional footballer, I had the option of going to university as I had received a distinction in my BTEC in sport, which most scholars take – which is enough to get you into higher education.

If I stayed in football to push for a pro contract at Spurs, I needed a back-up plan. Success is never guaranteed in any career. Although it takes drive, courage and hard work you also need that added ingredient – a smidgeon of luck.

I decided to push on in football, but I embarked on an Open University business studies degree which gave me something positive to do in my spare time and might enable me to get a decent job if football didn't work out.

The odds are statistically stacked against academy footballers. From my under 16s age group at Watford, at 26, only two players out of the 16 boys still play in the EFL, a few are playing non-League football but the rest have given up. It is a similar picture all over the country.

If you pondered these facts for too long, you'd quit on the spot. Uncertainty plays a big part of football but so too does opportunity. Progressing through the academy system is like a long race with dozens of hurdles to leap over. Some players peak early and fade, others never quite fulfil their early potential. You get late bloomers who come through the field but most fall at one hurdle or another. Only the rare few stay the whole course.

Between the ages of 16 to 22 it becomes much clearer who will have a career in the game. We develop physically and technically at different rates and unless you are truly talented it can be a constant grind to earn a succession of short-term contracts that offer little semblance of job security.

You can easily drop from being in a strong position – playing well and earning good money – to finding yourself released without any meaningful qualifications or job prospects. Then what? If you decide to go back into education, you're playing catch up behind everyone else.

To get a good job, you need work experience so are at the back of the queue there too. Having been in the football bubble for so long former players often struggle to cope with so called 'ordinary life.' It can take years to find your feet properly. Away from the world of work, playing sport let alone football can be difficult. It is why so many give the game up, and even stop playing sport, completely. The memories just hurt too much.

As the number of casualties rise of former players suffering with poor mental health and from harmful addictions, some sadly to the point of suicide, serious questions are at last being asked if clubs really do enough to provide players with the advice and support needed to adapt to a fresh phase of their lives once their careers are over.

In some respects, it is hard to blame academics because their business model is focused on developing one or two players a season for senior football. They – we – are assets. We can either make it to the first team and compete for the club or be sold for money the club can reinvest. But what about the boys who don't make it? Those who, to the clubs at least, suddenly have no value. What does the game do for them?

My biggest motivation was the fear of failure. Some people might perceive this to be a negative mindset but to me it was a driving factor. I was prepared to do all that was needed to achieve my dream. Once I overcame the disappointment of failing to win a professional contract, I realised my race was far from run. Yes, I could look for another club to offer me a professional contract or I could pack it all in and look to go onto university, but deep down I really wanted to carry on and convince Spurs I had what it took.

As I sat beside the pool on holiday that summer, I broke down the parts of the game that were relevant to my position:

Physical: Agility, Balance, Core, Diet, Flexibility, Fitness, Leg strength, Upper body strength.

Technical: Passing, Heading, Dribbling/running with the ball, Turning, Clearances, Footwork.

Others: Leadership, Will-to-win.

These were elements I either needed to improve or develop. The first list were attributes that could help me to execute the skills in the second list. The third list highlighted important facets of the game I needed to master to enhance my performance.

I then looked at each area in detail and wrote a plan that would enable me to develop each facet, each week. For areas like diet and nutrition, I committed to eating healthily and to stop drinking during the season. I needed to record and measure my results, so I set weekly, monthly, and annual goals and made sure that I reviewed them regularly.

For the forthcoming season my targets were:

- Win a pro contract
- Play in most reserve team games
- Train with the first team.

My short and medium-term goals focused on developing my game. My most important aim was to ensure I wouldn't find myself in the position I had at the end of the previous season again. The second was to never make excuses for anything and the third wasn't to blame anyone for anything bar myself. As the new pre-season began, I was prepared to work as hard as possible to win a professional contract as soon as possible.

Elsewhere, Loz started his first season as a professional at Spurs while Spenno began to adapt to part-time football with Wingate & Finchley and to find a job to supplement his income. Beau was off to uni and Jack was still on the road back to recuperation at Watford as, like me, he was now a third-year scholar.

Mason spent his summer going on trial at several Premier League and Championship clubs and also in Scotland and Spain, a broad mix he hoped would result in a contract offer.

Matt had returned from a summer break to find himself out of favour at Stevenage before he'd even turned up for training. He wasn't invited on the club's pre-season tour with the manager insisting he wanted Matt off the wage bill. Matt preferred to stay on to fight for his place but soon went on loan to Boreham Wood where he scored four goals in 21 matches.

I was pleased with my pre-season. I did well in all my fitness tests and impressed the first team coaches looking on. I was determined to show I could cope and become a standout player.

The first game of my season was against Chelsea whose youth team included my old Pegasus pal Alex Davey, although he didn't play in that game as Chelsea's central defensive partnership was Andreas Christensen, who is now a first team regular at Stamford Bridge and a Danish international, and Nathan Ake, who now plays for Manchester City.

Chelsea also had Nathaniel Chalobah, John Swift, Josh McEachran, Ruben Loftus-Cheek and Izzy Brown in their team – quality young players with promising futures, while we had Jordan Archer, Ryan Fredericks, Kevin Stewart, Nabil Bentaleb, Tom Carroll and a certain Harry Kane in our starting 11.

It was always going to be a close contest and I had an absolute blinder to carry on my good pre-season form in an impressive 4-2 win.

One day after training in mid-August, my coach Chris Ramsey asked me to join the other coaches for lunch in the canteen. They asked me how I thought I was doing. We all knew the answer. I was flying and was working my balls off to win a pro contract. My performances reflected that. They teased me for a while but eventually put me out of my misery. I was awarded my first professional contract for the remainder of the season. It was the most amazing feeling and a complete contrast to how I'd felt at the end of the previous season.

I'd achieved a dream I'd had since I was five years old. It had seemed such a tough journey, not least in the past two years, but I had finally got there and amid the joy there was also relief. I had finally been rewarded for my hard work.

This had nothing to do with money. At moments like this money doesn't matter regardless of how much people like to believe footballers are solely driven by it. Yes, it was nice to have my wages quadrupled but this was more about the prestige of becoming a fully-fledged professional footballer.

The first person I told was my dad. I ran outside, called him and he was as excited as I was, proud and, most importantly, pleased I had been rewarded for the hard work I had put in. I sensed he was starting to lose faith in my chances of making it. Parents are bound to think this way when they see their children experiencing disappointment. He had done everything possible to provide the opportunity for me to pursue my dream and now it was happening. I told the lads who were also buzzing for me.

The Spurs coaches even thought my form might earn a call up to England at under 19s level. I wasn't sure how this might work given that I was already playing for Northern Ireland, but I spoke to England under 19s manager, Noel Blake, who said they had watched me play, were impressed, and if I wanted to switch, he could start the process to change my allegiance.

It was always my dream to play for England so I gave him permission but knew it could be complicated. Northern Ireland had been great to me over many years. They had given me the chance to play international football, had made me captain of my age group and pushed me to join my brother at under 21 level.

England was different. I would be among the very top players in my age group so there was no way that I could turn that down. The call came just before the international break when I was due to play for Northern Ireland under 19s in the upcoming European Championships. I couldn't go on the trip if I was about to swap allegiance soon.

Respectfully I told my under 19 Northern Ireland coach, Stephen Craigan, of my decision and could hear the frustration in his voice in losing his captain so close to the championships. Michael O'Neill, Northern Ireland's first team manager, urged me to reconsider but my mind was made up. I duly signed the papers to finalise my decision.

Everything looked rosy. I'd had an incredible six months – just as I had in the first half of the previous season. Inexplicably, I then had another dip. In fact, I seemed to constantly have these good and bad spells. It wasn't laziness. I was a hard worker who didn't need a rocket up my backside but I was too intense at times and constantly needed to calm down and not worry too much or overthink things. It got to a stage where I put myself under so much pressure to meet my daily goals that I often went to bed feeling guilty. It was a lengthy old checklist which just got longer and longer and looks ridiculous in hindsight.

A typical day included visualisation, flexibility, core strength, training, extras (such as longer range passing), sharpness in the dome, lower body training with the team, foam roller exercises, ice bath, gym after dinner, upper body work, stretches, pool, daily review and meditation – 14 different things, mostly additions to my actual football training which, in itself, was tough going.

I can't explain why I did it. Conversely, for all my apparent overt professionalism and seriousness, I lurched back to excessive partying – often out until 4am which wrecked my body and undid the hard work I'd put in all week.

I had been in such a good place. After news of my England call up, I was at my absolute peak. No partying for six months, no staying out late, no eating junk food – but doubling my training which took its toll physically and mentally. I was exhausted, bored and, worst of all, lost the enjoyment I had for the game. I was exercising just so I could go to bed that night without feeling guilty. It left me knackered in training and feeling unmotivated football-wise.

It came to a head in a reserve game against Liverpool at St Helens' rugby league stadium. As I hadn't visualised the game properly for the previous two nights, in my mind I hadn't ticked all the boxes so went into the game expecting a catastrophe to happen.

It duly did. Midway through the first half I scuffed a back flick which sent the ball to their striker who raced past me to go one on one with our goalkeeper who, thankfully, made a save. It was a warning sign. By half-time we were 3-0 down. I had given a penalty away for their first goal with their second goal being my fault too after another stray pass. I couldn't have felt any smaller as I trudged back into the changing room at half time.

Our coach, Tim Sherwood, stood with his back to the wall opposite me, only a table between us. I had my hands on my head looking down at the floor. After a minute, I briefly popped my head up and caught a glimpse of his eyes. He was staring straight at me, his face red with rage. After two minutes he spoke, calmly at first, saying my name so I would lift my head.

'Dom? Dom, have you ever played football before?' I didn't respond. He tried again. 'Dom, seriously, it looks like you've never played football before. What were you doing out there?' Again, I said nothing. His voice got louder, his tone sharper. 'Dom, how the hell do you think you can play for your country because right now you couldn't get a game for the Faroe Islands?' He knew this would hit home. From the form I had been in when I was touted as a potential England player, right now, I wouldn't get into anyone's team.

It was tactical, of course. Sherwood knew I responded well to criticism. This was the worst game I had played so I deserved a rollicking. One thing you learn about managers and coaches is you don't need to worry if they batter you. It is when they stop trying to rile you that you should be concerned. Sherwood knew I was capable of better. My performance was unacceptable, and he wanted to make sure I knew it. If he hadn't said anything I would have been truly worried. I knew Sherwood still believed in me.

People outside the game might construe his comments to be over the top. In most workplaces, sarcasm and shouting are deemed as verbal abuse. In football, coaches and managers need to get players performing at their best. At this stage of my career, I wanted to play well for the reserves so I could start to challenge for the first team.

Dishonesty is a weak alternative. Perform the way I just had in the first team and it wouldn't just be a manager getting at you but fans and the media, maybe even your teammates whose careers you are placing in jeopardy.

You have to learn fast. I've had other hammerings before, but this was the worst and, looking back, I can smile now because I truly was that bad and deserved to be told in no uncertain terms. Secondly, I was given the chance to respond by playing the second half with the message ringing loud and clear. If this had been a first team match, I would have been hauled off and left to mull over my mistakes.

My second half was only marginally better than the first and I couldn't wait for the final whistle to blow so I could put the game behind me and move on. My intensity meant I would inevitably replay the game over and over in my head and focus on areas that needed improving to avoid making the same mistakes again.

That game had been coming. I had gone too far with my training programme and my mindset became obsessed more with my daily to-do list than enjoying my football. Hard work isn't always the answer and as I upped my personal programme my performances worsened and for a month or two I played with absolutely no confidence.

My evident drop in form and constant tiredness due to my late nights caused one of the coaches to call me at home to ask if I was taking drugs. He had seen it before and asked if that was the problem he would help. I laughed of course not – never had, never will – but it was the only rational explanation he could think of for my demise in form after such a storming start to the season. That really put things into perspective. I was being offered addiction advice with obsession being my real problem – I was just too stubborn to admit it.

Once again, I turned to the only solution I knew – hard work. I knocked going out on the head so my football would improve. I was fighting for another contract now and unless I wanted to find myself going on trial again, I had to persuade Spurs I was worth at least another year.

A couple of weeks later the same coach called to talk about my future. He thought it might be a good idea for me to check out some other clubs in case Spurs didn't offer me a new deal. To me, this was Tottenham saying it was unlikely I'd get a new contract beyond the current season. Just as I felt when I was released by Watford, a massive weight lifted from my shoulders. It no longer mattered how I trained or played – I could just enjoy myself again.

My agent, who I had signed with the previous year, arranged for me to go on trial to Bolton Wanderers, who were a good Championship side at the time. A change of scenery might be good. I also wanted a back-up option should Spurs decide to let me go. However, I didn't really enjoy my three-day trial even though they offered me a three-year deal which provided some much-needed security and a viable route to first team football.

Spurs reacted by offering me a one-year contract extension, suggesting they didn't want me to leave yet. It was great news. Deep down, I hadn't wanted to leave or sign for Bolton. It pushed Spurs into making a commitment which proved a catalyst for better days ahead.

My training improved and my performances got better. I played with more freedom and enjoyment and during the March international break I received the best news possible. I had been selected for the England under 19s squad for an upcoming game against Turkey.

What a whirlwind. In the space of a few weeks, I'd ditched my over training and excess partying amid fears of being released, received an option to join Bolton but been offered a new deal by Spurs and now I'd been called up to play for my country.

It was a proud moment. This time I held off calling my mum or dad so I could surprise them when I got home. It was a time to turn the music up loud in my car and sing all the way home. This was what football was all about – savouring the rewards of hard work and overcoming tears and disappointment to achieve a seemingly impossible dream of playing for England.

When I got home, mum was preparing dinner and dad was getting changed having just arrived home from work. I wanted to subtly drop my England call up into the conversation so they barely realised I had said it. As usual, as dad came downstairs he asked how my day had gone so I replied by saying it had been a normal day and that I had trained well. I pretended to walk out of the room then murmured I had also been called up the England under 19 squad.

'What was that?' asked Dad. 'I have been called up to play against Turkey for England.' Mum lifted her head and stopped preparing dinner. The shock on their faces was a picture. Dad congratulated me and gave me a big hug. Mum made a lovely comment and had a huge smile on her face. It felt so good to make them proud of me.

When I played for Northern Ireland, I usually went straight to the airport from the Spurs training ground to catch a flight to Belfast. On this occasion, I was chauffeured from home up to St George's Park in Staffordshire with Brandon Ormonde-Ottewill, a left back with Arsenal. The two-and-a-half-hour drive gave me time to get to know Brandon who I shared a room with. As newbies to the England squad, we met the rest of the team over dinner in the evening.

The sound of a knife striking a wine glass on our table as we finished dinner meant one thing – a song from the new boy. Soon I was stood on my chair crooning a rendition of the Robbie Williams song *Angels* to my new-found England teammates which included Callum Chambers, Callum Robinson, Lewis Baker, Harrison Reed, John Swift, Matt Targett, Isaac Hayden and Alex Mowatt – quality footballers I had played against many times. I received loud applause from all of them and our coaches and felt finally at ease having completed my initiation ceremony.

The standard of training throughout the week was incredibly high and I did my best to keep up. I started quietly but by the end of the week I was driving through the midfield and hitting diagonal passes to both wingers. I didn't start against Turkey but came on 10 minutes from time to make my England debut. So many people sent congratulations it felt good to be recognised as one of the best players for my age in the country.

The following season I played seven times for England's under 20s where I was fortunate to play, once again, alongside my old Pegasus teammate Harry Toffolo. We'd both come such a long way from those early days playing Saturday morning junior football. What an end to a topsy-turvy season.

CHAPTER 10

REALITY

T here is a view in football that you shouldn't have close friends in the game.

I couldn't disagree more. I get why people say it and what that means – and know some coaches favour a single-minded approach as they believe it can accelerate a player's progress, but it is easy to overlook the value of friendship. Yes, you need to focus on the task in hand and can't allow relationships to cloud your judgement, but we all need friends to share with at times.

Take the lads featured in this book and those mentioned as teammates. It is no surprise we bonded at such a young age – or how easy it was for people like Lawrence to join our circle of friends a little later in their academy journey. There was no masterplan, it just happened naturally. We shared the same passion and interests and enjoyed each other's company. It is called camaraderie which, to me, is a positive thing.

Despite the changing room banter and bravado, football can be a lonely profession at times. Fewer groups of people under the age of 30 move around as much as young footballers. There is a time and place for competition, but you need friends to share the experiences with, people who appreciate how you're feeling because they are going through the same things themselves.

At 18, I had a close group of friends who I had met through football and hoped to make many more. As our careers and our lives broadened, we were to have a myriad of quite different experiences.

Beau, for instance, had started his first year at university but soon found sports science hard going and not really something he wished to pursue. University football didn't float his boat either. The question was what would he do instead?

Jack was still on a long hard road back from his cruciate injury and hoped to return by Christmas. He was more motivated than ever with a single target in mind – to earn a professional contract.

After six years at Spurs, Mason understandably went through some tough times following his release by Tottenham and found trials at other clubs a challenging experience. Coming from a top club, it was easy enough to get trials but winning a contract proved a lot harder.

His first trial at Crystal Palace summed up the problem in a nutshell. Palace already had a highly rated young striker, Reise Allassani, who they had invested lots of time and effort into developing. Unless Mason could prove he was substantially better, he wouldn't be offered a contract. He couldn't so they didn't.

Mason's next trial was with Sporting Club Braga in Portugal, an unusual and potentially exhilarating opportunity which Spurs sourced for him at a fellow top European club. Mason was excited but apprehensive. If he succeeded, he would be living on his own in a foreign country unable to speak the language or see his family for months on end – a barrier and possibly overpowering reason why his trial failed.

Next, he ventured to Edinburgh for a trail with Hibernian, who decided against offering a contract leaving just one final, ultimately unsuccessful, trial at Hull City. With the doors closing, and feeling fed up and dejected, Mason lost the determination to carry on. It was hard for me to empathise as I didn't know how well he had performed and as my own trial experience had been so completely different. Mason had been to four clubs and hadn't received a single offer.

Like so many other players who suffer in silence, Mason would eventually struggle to come to terms for many years from his release from Tottenham and is only now truly starting come out the other side of it. During those years he kept his emotions bottled up, living life in something of a daze at times, unable to share his true feelings of rejection with anyone and certainly not wanting anyone's sympathy.

His experience is typical of so many other boys. Football was everything he had worked for and with it no longer there he found it hard to cope. He tried to put the disappointment to the back of his mind during his trials as he was desperate to rekindle the dream. That only increased the internal pressure he placed on himself though as he wanted to stay in the game so badly which meant he couldn't play freely. The more trials he had, the tenser he became, and the more pressure mounted until football was no longer the game he loved.

Each rejection sapped Mason's confidence. Hope isn't enough at this stage in a young player's career. Mason needed to go into every trial with a positive mindset. It didn't help that some of his mates like Loz and I seemed to be playing well and making progress.

There was another reason Mason needed to succeed. He no longer had an income so if he couldn't earn a profession as a footballer, he had to consider other options. During his schooldays Mason had focused mainly on his football. He didn't do well at school – his GCSE grades were mainly Cs and Ds – as he hadn't thought two years after leaving school he might need to rely on his education to help find a job.

It is the other side of the 'give your all to football' coin. What happens if you fail to make it as a professional footballer? The cosy, somewhat ignorant, assumption in the cosseted football bubble is that you can breezily bounce into any job you like in the so-called 'ordinary world' as if there isn't comparable competition among other professions as there is in football or that people don't fight just as hard to make it in other walks of life.

This is false. Those with the best skillsets, education and knowledge tend to come out on top. Mason's expertise was football. Let's not forget he was encouraged to spend one or two days a week during schooltime training with Spurs. He lived in the moment. Like hundreds of young players who leave the game each year the thought of a 'real job' seemed crazy. We're all going to become professional footballers, right? Every nod of approval fortifies that belief. Failure isn't an option.

You don't fail in being unable to succeed in football – the air is just too rare for those who leave the game each year and there are too few opportunities available for them. Mason wasn't just behind his peers – he had never written a CV, had no work experience, too little real education yet needed to find a job to earn money like everyone else.

In an attempt to resurrect his career, Mason dipped into local semi-professional non-League football, initially playing for local Southern League team, Hitchin Town, then Hemel Hempstead Town, which was even closer to where he lived, who played in the Conference South (now National League South), the sixth tier of English football. Maybe that would work?

After Christmas, Jack finally returned to training. It had taken longer than expected but complicated injuries like Jack's are rarely straightforward.

Lawrence had a solid six months in the reserves with me at Spurs but being a year older he too needed to go out on loan to get some first team football under his belt.

Loan moves are a big part of most young players development. We were now 19 or 20 year olds and like most players in top flight academies were ready for our first real taste of senior first team football, usually among the gritty reality of the lower leagues.

Loz dipped even further down going to Hyde (now Hyde Town) who were at the foot of the National League (tier five of English football). A six-month loan move there provided the opportunity to get plenty of games under his belt and offer a good grounding in tough senior football – the hardest physically he's ever played according to Loz, let alone as a 20-year-old.

Jack struggled to get back after his injury after such a long time out. His knee wasn't the same and he couldn't regain full fitness. He lost confidence and couldn't do the things he once found so easy. Time is such a critical factor for young players. You can't afford to be out of the game for a whole year at that stage of your career as clubs have difficult decisions to make – not least with other players vying for the same place.

Although he had been at Watford since he was seven, Jack was released after 12 years at the club at the end of the season – not because he didn't work hard or wasn't good enough but because he had been unlucky with injury. It seemed such a cruel blow. Jack had just four months after his return from injury to show he was worth a contract, which proved an impossible task. Ideally, he needed much longer – possibly another year to regain his fitness. By then, other cohorts of players will have come through.

Like it or not, football is a business and clubs see players as assets. Once you lose your value, you become an expense – a liability the club can ill afford. Jack's situation was no different to hundreds of other players each season who have to fight back from injury whether they are an academy player aiming to win a first contract or a seasoned pro seeking an extended deal. If you can't prove your worth, you're out. Jack now had to get his knee into good shape so he could win a contract elsewhere.

Having not enjoyed it, Beau decided to quit his course at the end of his first year at university. Instead, he began working with a friend who had set up a go-ahead new business called New Curious Generation, a marketing agency specialising in a somewhat novel mix of digital marketing and merchandising, including leather-bound notebooks and journals, which he found more interesting and enjoyable than playing football or studying at university. It was the end of Beau's football journey and his Premier League dream.

The following 2014-15 season began with lots of movement among the lads.

Spenno moved from Wingate & Finchley to Bishop Stortford Town, who played in the same league but were a slightly bigger club. It seemed a small step up and a good move at first sight. Although he was on more money, he soon found the time consuming three-hour round trip twice a week and additional petrol costs nullified any financial benefit to the move. When the opportunity to move to a team closer to home popped up, he took it. Still contracted to Bishop's Stortford, he spent the rest of the season on loan at Harrow Borough.

Back from his experience at Hyde, Loz, now aged 20, faced another problem that is unique to football. A game of opinions, Tottenham's goalkeeping coach Tony Parks preferred a different young goalkeeper at the club so Loz was released by Spurs.

Fortunately, Alex Inglethorpe who had been our youth team coach at Spurs, became academy manager at Liverpool FC and offered Loz an amazing opportunity to move to the north-west.

He had excelled under Alex at Spurs and seemed to be the perfect goalkeeper to implement his football philosophy, which was to build from the back. A technically sound goalkeeper, Loz could also pass the ball with accuracy. I loved playing with him because, as a defender, I knew any time I wanted the ball he would give it to me. If I came under pressure, he would accept the ball back just as readily. His incredible rise from college football to one of the biggest clubs in the world as a professional footballer in less than three years was truly inspiring. Despite being away from his family, Loz just couldn't miss the opportunity to join Liverpool and recalls how good they were at helping him as a young player settle in.

He spent his first season in Liverpool's reserve team competing with their other goalkeepers and amassing plenty of experience among quality players.

By contrast, Mason struggled to get to grips with life after academy football. He didn't feature much for Hemel Hempstead Town so moved to Kings Langley, which didn't work out either.

He'd initially enjoyed playing football free from the demands of top end academy football. It felt like being a kid again. But Mason found the standard of football to be poor, a situation that wasn't helped by terrible pitches which were a world away from the pristine surfaces we were used to playing on in academies. Now working 10-hour days with his dad, he also had to juggle training sessions and games around the new world of work which he found tiring. It takes time to adjust to this new double world of work so by matchday on Saturdays or on weekday evenings he would be absolutely knackered.

The transition from playing with technically gifted players on carpet-like pitches to rutted non-League surfaces can be hard to handle too. In non-League football, often by necessity, the ball is hoofed around with a reliance on physical contact to win or keep the ball often at the expense of skill. It isn't the football we were groomed to play.

Ready to give the game up completely, Mason decided to give it one final go at Welwyn Garden City FC, who play in Southern League Division One Central (the eighth tier of English football).

Mason started the season well and bagged a few goals but once again found himself out of favour and back on the subs bench in preference to players with a more full-on attitude to the game. Some, he felt, were picked because they were the manager's mates rather than for their ability. Mason lost his way and couldn't adapt. While some ex-academy players turn their careers around in non-League football, Mason is far from being alone among former academy players to wonder about what the future may hold and to decide whatever it is, this wasn't it. Football moved down the pecking order.

Jack's search for a new club also proved difficult. The world is no longer your oyster if you are released as a teenage footballer. The Premier League has gradually evolved from one dominated by home grown players to a league that now attracts the best players from around the world. With such high stakes and big money involved, Premier League clubs are prepared to spend huge sums of money on tried and tested internationals rather than give young players the time and space to grow into the role. England's second tier, the Championship, is going much the same way.

Academies increasingly look to polish the occasional rare diamond with the ability to become a world class star to play for their first team and who, when the time is right, they can sell for astronomical sums of money that will fund their academy for years, maybe even decades, to come.

The future for most former Premier League academy graduates is less aspirational. Their only viable route to a professional career is usually a downwards move to the Championship or lower. The choice is rarely in their hands as clubs release talented young players and sell them on to recoup the running costs of their academies.

It is a domino effect. Each time a player moves downwards a player at that level is released – which is a disincentive for smaller clubs seeking to develop their own home grown players if they can buy players cheaper than the cost and effort of running their own academy. It is equally easy to recruit players from overseas, squeezing opportunities for home grown players even tighter. A report commissioned by the Professional Footballers' Association in 2008 called Meltdown predicted this gloomy conclusion. It is becoming eerily true.

No club will sign an injured player so Jack wasn't even aspiring to find a Premier League or Championship club, just anywhere he could play and get back to full fitness. When nothing emerged in England, Watford arranged a move to Spanish club, Cadiz. He then moved to a club in Gibraltar which worked well as it offered him an opportunity to get his knee back to full strength and be paid at the same time so he could potentially win a contract at an English League club.

Trouble is, lower league clubs aren't looking for good reserve players, they need players who are ready for first team action. Oxford United offered an extended trial but weren't quite convinced. With it looking unlikely he would get a professional Football League contract, Jack joined Hemel Hempstead Town where Spenno and Mason had also played. Strange as it sounds, having played overseas, Jack had to wait three months for international clearance which swallowed up the rest of the season. Another setback.

My bother Matt was released by Stevenage after his contract ran out in the summer of 2014. He hadn't lost his love of football but couldn't wait to get away from the professional game which he felt had beaten him up and spat him out. He didn't want to deal with the see-saw of emotions anymore so signed for non-League Farnborough FC, where he had been on loan from Stevenage, seeing it as a chance to reset.

With Beau and Mason having given up and Jack seemingly on his way out too, the only certainty among many of our group of friends was uncertainty.

CHAPTER 11

AND THEN THERE WERE FOUR...

My own 2014-15 pre-season began well. Mauricio Pochettino came in as Spurs manager and was prepared to offer opportunities to younger players. In September, he asked me to join the first team squad in preparation for a Europa League game in Greece against Asteras Tripolis. I was absolutely buzzing to be travelling with the first team for the first time.

We flew by private jet to Greece and I wore a Spurs suit for the first time so felt on top of the world. However, I was canny enough to park as far as possible from the variety of Range Rovers and similar sized vehicles driven by the established first team players at the airport car park. My small BMW 2 series car was nice, but not in their league.

I realise this is meaningless one-upmanship but that's the world you enter as a senior Premier League pro. Our academy manager warned me the club's management hated seeing young players drive flashy cars. It was a sign they thought they'd already made it.

This was another step up following my England experience and the first time I felt like a proper senior professional footballer. I didn't make the bench for the match, but it was good to be among the first team.

As I walked out of the players' tunnel ahead of the game, the TV cameras turned and pointed straight at me. I didn't know where to look as it was my first time in this sort of environment, so I just tried to appear as composed as possible. The Europa League flag covered the centre circle and the home fans sang their hearts out as both teams warmed up. I realised more than ever this was what I wanted every week and I was gutted not be playing. I was close, very close, to being the first among our group to achieve the elusive dream of playing in the Premier League.

A few weeks later I travelled with the squad to play Hull City in the Premier League. Spurs had a few players injured so I knew I stood a decent chance of getting a game and was on the subs bench. We were favourites to win but came away with a disappointing draw – not that it diminished the excitement at being a sub in my first Premier League game. Even closer.

I couldn't have asked for a better start to the season but knew I needed to keep the momentum going to realise my dream. After the Hull game a few other reserve players joined the first team squad, including the highly rated Harry Winks, who has since fulfilled his promise by becoming a full England international, and Joshua Onomah, considered to be the best player in Tottenham's academy at the time, who now plays for Fulham.

Both were midfielders who had consistently played in teams above their age group so were able to adapt to first team training. By comparison, I couldn't maintain the same consistency. I knew I wasn't quite ready for it and eventually Pochettino dropped me back to the reserves with no obvious plan for me to return to the first team any time soon.

One of the sports scientists delivered the news that my time with the first team was up. I wasn't embarrassed because I had done my best. This was the highest possible level I could have reached for now. I would only move back up if they felt I had improved.

I returned to training with the reserves on a rollercoaster of emotions. Just because I wasn't ready as a 19-year-old to play in the Premier League it didn't mean I wouldn't return at some point in the future. The club gave me the long-term chance to develop by offering a two-and-a-half-year deal. This was the stability I strived for so was fantastic news even if I was in a quandary.

Although the rest of my mates featured in this book would have loved to be offered anything remotely like this, I was in limbo land between being a good reserve team player but not quite good enough for the first team.

As New Year loomed, I reflected on a crazy calendar year which had started with me putting myself under too much pressure, drinking to excess when I went out with my mates, losing form, being told I was likely to be released, then being offered an optional three-year deal at Bolton, improving again, getting a call up for England, promoted to the Spurs first team and getting on the first team bench twice, offered a new and improved long-term contract but now dropped back to the reserves and looking possibly to go out on loan. A big second half of the season beckoned.

With such a lack of stability it is small wonder so many young players are riddled with self-doubt and insecurity. Even if they become fully fledged professionals the chances are they stop enjoying football and just start to see it as a job.

As you have read with Beau, Jack and Mason's experiences, the professional game can be tough to progress to – but once you are there like Loz, Spenno, Matt and me there are so many concerns such as relegation, injury, being dropped for months on end, living away from home, struggling financially and not knowing when the next wage packet is coming in. These are all reasons footballers fall out of love with the game. Young players can also lack the patience to deal with a hiatus in their progress or turbulence on the journey. To me, these are all ingredients that can lead to poor mental health which is so familiar in modern professional football.

In recent years our increased awareness of these issues among sportsmen and women has seen players feel confident to step forward and talk honestly about their personal experience of depression. People only see footballers enjoying success when they are on TV, winning games, celebrating goals and lifting trophies – getting high on the highs.

What people don't see are when they get low on the lows. The addictions to gambling, drink, drugs and countless other distractions not to mention the lack of sleep caused by worry and the modern phenomena of sitting at home scrolling through their Twitter feed to check the online abuse after a poor performance.

The reality is footballers are vulnerable to depression because while money might bring a level of happiness, it can't guarantee it. Young players go through so much uncertainty in the early stages of their career they can become damaged goods later in life.

Each of the lads featured in this book has suffered to one degree or another. Okay, life isn't easy and is rarely fair. We get that too. But in football, the highs and lows are constant. You can play the best game of your life on a Saturday but break your leg on a cold Tuesday night. You can lurch from confidence and kudos to nine months out of action, in physical pain punctuated only by sessions on the physio's table and the excruciating mental stress of not knowing what the future holds.

I was a classic example. When I had a good game, I felt on top of the world and would go out partying with my mates. I then became over-confident going into the next game and maybe try things out I wouldn't normally attempt. After a bad game, I'd feel like the worst player in the world and would worry about it for days.

I knew I needed help so I was put in touch with Jag Shoker, a performance coach who specialised in psychology. Jag worked with John Obika, who was older than me in the reserves at Spurs at the time and had an exceptionally powerful positive presence and energy. Within five minutes I knew he was the guy I needed. I felt I could be honest in ways I hadn't been able to with any of the coaches I had worked with. The meeting wasn't just about me getting a feel for Jag but the other way around too. He wanted to see what I was like and if I was coachable. I felt I could trust him, so we met every two weeks for a couple of hours which I saw as a necessary investment in my career.

Jag taught me to neutralise my emotions. It helps to remember that just as you don't become a good player overnight, you don't become a bad one either. The only thing that changes is how you see yourself in relation to the position you are in. If you believe you have become a bad player, you will start to act like one.

Mason, for example, hadn't suddenly become a poor footballer but let the circumstances he was in become too much. In January, he decided to hang up his boots having been unable to adapt to football after leaving the academy system. Non-League football just didn't cut it for Mason. Only playing in fits and starts, he was sat on the bench most weeks which pretty much took up all his Saturdays – time he could spend relaxing or going out with his mates after a physically tough working week. Like Beau a year earlier, for my oldest football mate, it was the end of the road for his football career. We were down to four.

I was at a crossroads too. Despite the apparent security of a long term contract, I knew I had to prove myself to Spurs so I went out on loan for the first time, joining League Two Cambridge United, which was just a 40-minute drive from our family home. With little opportunity at Spurs, I needed to get some first team games under my belt.

Cambridge's training ground was at a cricket club where I met the manager and players for the first time and a wholly difference experience to arriving at Tottenham's multi-million-pound complex. I was delighted to play anywhere to help my development and although I had been playing as a centre-back at Spurs, I went to Cambridge to play in midfield because my skinny six-foot, one-inch frame wasn't yet ready for the physicality of League Two football.

It is a fundamental dichotomy of the loan system. What the loanee wants to develop his career doesn't necessarily match what the club bringing the player in needs to improve their situation.

My senior debut came in a 1-1 draw against Dagenham & Redbridge – a game we were expected to win. I did okay, enough to keep my place in the team for the next match, but felt I could have done better. Youth team football is often more technical than physical so to meet the demands of the more competitive games I planned to slowly build myself into matches and tried not to do anything too fancy until the game progressed. This didn't really work as 30 minutes went by with me only touching the ball a few times. I spent most of the game looking skyward as the ball was hoofed back and forth over my head.

My second game at Cambridge was a 10,000 capacity sell out away at our local rivals, Luton Town. The match started frenetically with players from both teams flying into tackles. During that chaotic first 15 minutes I only touched the ball once and didn't make a single challenge.

Luton took control and ran us ragged. Although I got gradually into the game, by half time we were 3-0 down and I was substituted. Although we pulled two goals back in the second half and lost 3-2, I had been a midfield passenger in a fierce game in which Luton ran all over us. I needed to be more assertive. The manager questioned our desire and courage as a team, words at Spurs which had a different meaning as they were used to measure your willingness to receive the ball, even if a player was marking you tight, and your passion to do something useful with it. Here it meant shouting, dominating headers and winning tackles.

It isn't how you envisage your professional career will be. You might expect an 'all for one, one for all' spirit among your teammates but loan players are often viewed as little more than temporary but necessary cover. No one cares if you're gaining valuable experience to progress your career – not least fans who just want their team to win. You can appreciate that and understand you're unlikely to truly be one of the lads for long so are barely worth getting to know among your teammates. In fact, you might even be taking their best mate's place in the team, a long-standing colleague who may have to move on or downwards or may be in danger of losing their career completely.

This wasn't a great introduction to first team football. I found myself on the subs bench for the next six weeks, not even coming on as a substitute. I was fed up and with ten games left in the season badly needed some football. I trained hard but had lost the manager's trust in those opening 45 minutes at Luton. I didn't want my season to fade away so asked my reserve coach back at Tottenham, Ugo Ehiogu, if I could return to play a reserve game to maintain my match fitness. He agreed if Cambridge okayed it.

Before training on Thursday morning, I spoke to the manager to say as it was unlikely that I would play in Saturday's game as I wanted to play for Spurs reserves on Monday. He went ballistic and responded angrily by insisting he needed me for Saturday's match and didn't want me to play in the reserve game. I repeated my request after training, which felt a bit like pestering but felt I needed to say something as I was desperate for some game time.

Then I said something completely stupid. I told him I was ready and if he played me on Saturday, I guaranteed we would win the game. The arrogance of youth, eh? No footballer can ever pledge to win a match single-handed, let alone one the manager didn't even trust. He could have laughed in my face. Instead, he sat back in shock at something so ridiculous. I wanted him to know I was willing to fight for my shirt. Fitness aside, there was no benefit to me going back to play for Spurs reserves. I just needed first team action and was raring to go. I had done all I could to convince the manager I was ready and had nothing to lose by letting him know I was motivated and determined to turn things around.

It worked. Okay, maybe the first choice right back being out injured forced the manager's hand, but he put me straight in the side even though I hadn't played in that position before. We won 1-0 and I played a blinder. I worked so hard my legs cramped and I was taken off after about 70 minutes, but I had regained the manager's trust and played in each of the last nine games of the season, a run which helped us stay in the league with some solid performances along the way.

In the final away game of the season at Oxford United, one of their players caught me late with a nasty challenge. I was badly injured which robbed me of the chance to compete in the Toulon tournament – a major annual international competition for national youth teams including England under 20s.

I played seven times for England under 20s under Aidy Boothroyd that season including victories against Germany, Romania and the USA. We didn't lose a game that season and when I pulled on that England shirt I immediately felt like a top player.

At the end of a tumultuous season, I returned to Spurs having completed my first loan spell with 11 first team appearances under my belt, was now an England under 20s regular and had turned what was looking to be a terrible season into a good one. I had taken my first step on the ladder of first team football and had an appetite for more.

Two of us were still in League football, two were playing semi pro and two had given up completely.

My brother Matt had moved to Wealdstone in National League South from Farnborough during the season and decided to set up his own coaching company with a fellow player, Matty Bevans. He also began coaching at Boreham Wood FC on a youth development scheme for non-League clubs called PASE – the Programme of Academic and Sporting Excellence. More than anything else Matt seemed to rediscover his appetite for the game among the camaraderie of semi-pro non-League football.

None of us had played in the Premier League. What would our fourth season in full time football bring?

From Winning Teams to Broken Dreams

CHAPTER 12

THE LOAN RANGER

At the start of the 2015-16 season only Loz and I were left playing full time professional football.

Of the rest, Jack was now playing for Chesham and Spenno for Harrow Borough – both in non-League semi pro football – with Mason and Beau having hung up their boots completely and now working full-time – Mason for his dad and Beau still with New Curious Generation marketing agency.

The new season saw Lawrence and I go out on loan once again to get more experience under out belts.

With Liverpool having three good quality 'keepers in front of him at Anfield – Simon Mingnolet, Brad Jones and Danny Ward – Loz joined League One Swindon Town on loan with fellow Liverpool players Jordan Williams and Kevin Stewart for a whole season.

Again, the move came at a moment's notice. Loz was shopping with his wife and baby in the Trafford Centre in Manchester when he received a call ordering him to go straight to Swindon. He went home to collect some things, dropped his wife and child at the train station so they could return to London and drove down to Swindon for a day's training ahead of a pre-season friendly against West Brom on the Saturday. Ironically Loz's next game was a sell-out home match against Liverpool. He signed for Swindon for the season.

I completed another pre-season at Spurs, traversing between the first team and reserves. Each day, I'd see other players go out on-loan and was disappointed that no one was asking for me. I was still living at home and things got tense.

Selfishly, I let my frustration out on my family by becoming arrogant – an attitude I'd always hated in others, carrying the unworthy swagger we had been encouraged to show as footballers to let others know that nothing was going to get in our way. It is a fine line between the ego you need to play well and confidence, the surefootedness required for competent performances.

I was lucky to be told straight by my parents that my attitude was unacceptable. I had always tried to be a generous and kind person but had morphed into this mean-spirited, selfish monster who wouldn't listen to anyone and didn't do anything for anyone else bar my own self-interest. This was far worse than having a poor game. When the people that mean the most to you can't stand you because of what you have become then it is time to change. To me, being a good person is better than being a decent footballer.

With less than a week to go before the transfer window closed, I knew I needed to secure a move. One of my team-mates, Nathan Oduwa, was going on loan to a Scottish club and asked if I wanted to join him. This didn't sound like the greatest of options until I heard the name of the club. Glasgow Rangers FC, commonly known as Rangers.

My eyes lit up. This was a massive club like few others. Significantly, I had worked under their manager before. Mark Warburton had just taken over as manager at Rangers and had been my academy manager at Watford so I knew playing for him at Ibrox would be an incredible experience. I also had a long conversation with Ugo Ehiogu, Spurs under 23s coach who had been an England international defender and had played briefly for Rangers among many other clubs including Aston Villa, Middlesbrough and Sheffield United. The move made sense even though it was a big commitment to leave my family, friends and girlfriend behind.

Only when I arrived in Glasgow did I fully appreciate just how big Rangers are – that it isn't so much a football club, more a way of life. Fans are brought up to believe that football is the most important thing in the world, and Rangers the most important club. Their infamous rivalry with Celtic is burnt into the identity of each club and the fabric of Glaswegian life. You are either blue or green with no shades of grey.

On my first morning, I was shown around the training ground and ushered into a press conference where I sat in front of a table covered with microphones as if I was some sort of important signing of public interest. I had only done a couple of one-to-one interviews before, so this was completely different. As cameras clicked, I was quizzed by the assembled reporters, which tested my knowledge of the club's history. Other than garbling some sweeping generalisations about being pleased to be there I was found wanting.

In truth, I didn't appreciate the depth of Rangers' history so needed to get to grips with it smartish. I met John Brannagan, who was an informal player liaison for new boys and became a great friend. He showed me around the city and introduced me to some people who helped make my stay more enjoyable.

The following morning my interview was plastered all over the back pages of the Scottish newspapers. Rangers initially put me up in a hotel in the centre of Glasgow before finding me an apartment in the West End. Every time I ventured out Rangers fans would ask for a selfie, signature, or both. Back home, I was a nobody. Here I was a celebrity. The whole city knew me, and I hadn't even kicked a ball yet.

My loan spell at Rangers surpassed any expectations I may have had. Rangers were on their way back to the top after being dumped into the Scottish Second Division for financial irregularities in 2012 and having won back-to-back promotions in the previous two seasons were competing in the Scottish Championship with the aim of making it three promotions in a row to secure a return to the Scottish Premier League.

My teammates were great in training. It only took a few weeks to get up to speed with the standard. We had a big, strong squad with Gedion Zelalem, a German player with Arsenal, completing a trio of loan players who had moved up from the Premier League alongside Nathan and myself. We also signed Martin Waghorn from Sunderland and had veteran striker Kenny Miller upfront. Both would score more than 20 goals that season. It was always going to be a third straight promotion winning season and we led the table from start to finish.

I sat on the bench for the first two months as the team won their first 10 games in a row. Unsurprisingly, Warburton stuck with a winning team, but I felt I needed to let him know of my desperation to play.

Following my experience at Cambridge, I opted for a proactive approach so knocked on his door and told him I wanted a start. I only sat in my chair for about 20 seconds before walking straight back out. Mark knew me well from our Watford days and realising I was a bright boy told me in no uncertain terms that regardless of how well I may or may not have been doing in training, the team was on a winning streak so wouldn't be changed any time soon. He gave me a look as if to say, 'Dom, you're better than that'. I knew it was a daft question the moment the words left my lips. Of course, I wouldn't be in the team just yet unless there was an injury or dip in someone's form. I would have to be patient and wait for my chance. Nonetheless I had let him know of my desire. Never a bad thing.

It was all part of growing up, of course. With freedom came the responsibility of having to cook, wash and clean and pay all sorts of bills I didn't even know existed. Sat on the sofa one day a man knocked at my door and asked if I had paid my TV licence. I had never heard of it before so I rang my dad who couldn't believe it hadn't been paid. How was I supposed to know I needed a licence to watch TV?

Finally, I got my chance to play for Rangers. My first game at Rangers' home ground, Ibrox, was the stuff of dreams – walking out to 50,000 die-hard fans singing the Blue Sea of Ibrox at the top of their voices with their arms aloft was enough to bring out goosebumps and send a massive wave of adrenaline coursing through my body and every other Rangers player for that matter.

You feel like you are floating on a bed of air – being literally supported throughout the whole game. The most I had played in front of before was 10,000 and now I would be performing in front of five times that number, almost all of them backing me and my teammates to the hilt. There really is no feeling like it.

After a short run in the team, I was dropped over the Christmas period and put back in towards the end of January in a different position as a holding midfielder (a link between defence and midfield). As we played expansive football, sometimes we left ourselves exposed at the back and our results took a slight dip. Even though we were well on top in matches, we'd stopped scoring and other teams were being clinical on the break and scoring against us. We only scored one goal in a run of five games and then had a run of high scoring games in which we conceded three goals in four of the next five games.

I had done well for the first half of the season but the new role I was given took my game to a different level. It was where I should have played all along and a position I was ideally suited to. The next four months were the best of my career, including the most memorable match I have played so far, and culminated with me picking up three medals.

That said, I didn't play every game. The manager opted for a more attacking formation against some of the lesser teams in our league which meant we needed one less midfielder, so I was left out of these matches and kept fresh for games against teams in the top half of the table and for cup ties. I gained a lot of confidence and the fans took to me too. They even a song for me. It was the first time during my career that I felt like a proper professional footballer and the way I had envisioned it in my head as a young boy.

The final month of the season was unbelievable. We were well on course to win the league and had a big lead over Hibernian who were in second place. We also had a run in the Scottish Cup and having beaten Kilmarnock and Dundee, who were in the top six of the SPL, we faced our Auld Firm rivals Celtic in a semi-final at Hampden Park.

Rangers had struggled for many years and were one last step away from being back in the SPL where the club belonged. Celtic and Rangers had barely played each other in five years and while Rangers worked their way back up the leagues Celtic tightened their grip on virtually every competition.

Scottish football needs the Auld Firm rivalry and without those four annual matches (each team plays home and away twice in the SPL) it just hadn't been the same. The day of the Scottish Cup semi-finals draw was a major event and our team assembled in the canteen after training to hear the draw. Celtic were drawn out first and we waited in eager anticipation and the hope our name would be drawn out next. It duly was – Celtic v Rangers in the Cup semi-final. We celebrated and I was absolutely buzzing. My phone was busy all day and my dad immediately booked family flights up for the game. As a team, we had bags of confidence, and this was our toughest challenge of the season. We were expected to win the league, but the real yardstick of Rangers' comeback would be gauged by our performance against Celtic.

There was an interminable six-week build-up to the match. Every interview or article written about us inevitably mentioned the Celtic semi-final. We had to focus on more pressing matters with five league games scheduled before the semi-final with a 1-0 win against Dumbarton at Ibrox sealing promotion back to the SPL. Five days later we lifted the Scottish Challenge Cup final (called the Petrofac Trophy at the time – a competition for Scottish League clubs outside the SPL, including the top two Highland League clubs) with a resounding 4-0 victory against Peterhead at Hampden Park.

We met the night before the Celtic semi-final at Mar Hall Hotel on the outskirts of Glasgow. The nerves began to build and after dinner I wasn't relishing trying to sleep that night. Some of the lads asked for a sleeping pill and although I had never taken one before I joined them and consequently slept for 10 hours solid and woke up feeling amazing.

We were up bright and early as the game was a midday kick off. Despite this being by far the biggest game of my career, I felt quite relaxed safe in the knowledge I'd prepared the best I could. The game would take care of itself despite the magnitude of our task.

When we reached Hampden Park 90 minutes before the game thousands of Rangers fans surrounded the stadium to cheer the arrival of our coach. The pre-match atmosphere when we came out for the warm-up was like nothing I had experienced before. Both sets of fans had already filled the stadium. After the warm-up, Mark Warburton assembled us in a team huddle for his final speech. We had faith in one other with each player believing we could win. Warburton is one of the game's thinkers. He came to football late after a career in the City of London so is more philosophical about things than most. He stressed the need to perform well but also to enjoy the game and let the result take care of itself. We were up against the best team in Scotland, crammed with seasoned internationals and favourites to win. He asked us to play with freedom and confidence but most of all to prove we could compete with our age-old rivals.

Standing in the tunnel, I was determined to take everything in and the atmosphere as we walked on to the pitch was something I doubt I'll ever experience again. One side of the ground was blue, the other green. I looked around and savoured every moment. I barely heard the referee's whistle as we kicked off and I was hesitant at first as the game began without any real pattern. My brief was simple – to keep possession and protect our back four – a critical role as Celtic were experts at breaking quickly. I needed to impose myself and I got the perfect opportunity early on.

Five minutes in, I went for a 50/50 challenge with Celtic captain Scott Brown, a notoriously combative and highly experienced midfielder. I sprinted into a tackle just outside our penalty area to win the ball but also left Brown tumbled on the deck which earned big cheers from the Rangers fans. They knew the significance of a young player showing he could physically match up to Celtic's talisman – a player capable of controlling the game if allowed. To people who don't understand football it can sound a bit crude to leave an opponent on the deck, but it was a fair challenge and I knew Brown would soon respond given half a chance. I had shown I was ready to stand firm and in the opening skirmishes we fared well as we took the game to Celtic.

We took the lead in the 16th minute. Celtic cleared one of our attacks which I retrieved and played a square pass to Andy Halliday who skimmed a low cross into the box. Brown slid after the ball but diverted it into the path of Kenny Miller, our veteran striker and Brown's equivalent in terms of reputation and experience of Auld Firm clashes, who swept it into the net from close range. Our fans erupted and Kenny, with the whole team in close pursuit, ran the length of the pitch to celebrate with our fans. Confidence coursed through our team and try as they might Celtic could only muster a few half chances for the rest of the first half.

We knew Celtic would come out a different side after the break and so they did, piling on pressure immediately by winning four corners in five minutes then scoring with a header from Erik Sviatchenko. Other teams might have wilted but we didn't allow our heads to drop and kept trying to outplay them. I got booked in the 60th minute for grabbing an opponent after I'd lost control of the ball. Two minutes from normal time one of our centre backs, Rob Kiernan, went down injured and was substituted by Gedion Zelalem, a midfielder, which meant I had to drop back into defence to mark Leigh Griffiths, who was the best striker in Scotland at the time.

I was determined not to let him have a sniff and as the game went into extra time the tempo of the game dropped as everyone tired. We stayed solid at the back to make sure Celtic didn't score and regained the lead with a wonder goal from our winger, Barry McKay, six minutes into extra time, who picked the ball up 30 yards and skipped past Brown to smash the ball into the top corner.

It was the best goal I had ever seen in a game I had played in. Now 2-1 up in extra time, the celebrations were crazy but we needed to keep our heads and did exactly that to take our lead into half-time. Once again, Celtic hit back within seconds of the restart as Tomas Rogic swept in Kieran Tierney's low cross. Celtic now had the momentum. We had to hold on for the last 10 minutes and were happy to see the referee blow the final whistle.

Now we had the real test of nerves. Penalties. Warburton had the unenviable task of choosing our five penalty takers with pretty much everyone putting themselves forward including me, although I knew I would be well down the list so it was unlikely I would take one if it went to sudden death. Our team gathered on the halfway line as the shoot-out commenced.

Momentum rocked one way then the other. Andy Halliday scored first for us with Charlie Mulgrew replying for Celtic. Our full back James Tavernier then fired over but Callum McGregor hit the bar for Celtic to keep the shoot-out score 1-1. Barrie McKay converted to put us back in front, but Nir Bitton replied for Celtic.

Two penalties apiece and two to go. Now the pressure was truly on. Both goalkeepers came to the fore. Celtic's Craig Gordon saved Nicky Clark's penalty and our 'keeper, Wes Foderingham, then stopped Scott Brown's penalty. Lee Wallace converted for us with Leigh Griffiths replying for Celtic to make it 3-3 and take it to sudden death.

When Gedion Zelalem and Nicky Law scored our next two penalties with Mikael Lustig netting for Celtic, I felt anxious that I would have to take a penalty. But then Tom Rogic, Celtic's star player, stood up and…missed. Badly. Firing the ball well over the bar.

We'd won. As per usual for winners of penalty shoot-outs, our whole team sprinted towards our 'keeper but Wes somehow managed to side swerve us all and raced back to celebrate with the Rangers fans. Cartoon-like, (you could almost imagine a banjo playing rapidly in the background!), we followed in hot pursuit screaming as loud as we could in sheer delight only stopping for a brief group hug before running over to our fans.

I shared an emotional hug with the manager, coaches and anyone who was in my way before going over to our fans and to look for my family and friends in the crowd. It was the stuff of dreams. The pandemonium didn't stop for about ten minutes as everyone hugged and screamed. As things calmed down, I spotted my friends at the front being squished by everyone. As I went to hug them, I was embraced by about 20 people. It was crazy and I barely noticed my girlfriend, Jess, stood just a few metres away, her body half leant over the barrier. It was the most amazing moment, having just beaten Celtic, in front of people who were closest to me. Over 100 million viewers watched worldwide but nothing meant more than having my family and friends there.

We walked around the pitch for another 30 minutes as the Rangers fans continued to sing and my arms were sore with constantly applauding their support. Eventually we made our way back into the changing room. The manager spoke briefly and it took us a while to get onto our team coach and back to the training ground with my time taken up scrolling through my Twitter feed which had gone nuts with messages from so many people and pretty much every Rangers fan congratulating me and praising my performance.

There was a downside to take the edge off the day. On the coach, a teammate reminded me I couldn't play in the final as I had picked up yellow cards in the quarter and semi-finals so was suspended. I couldn't believe it. It must be one of the worst rules in football as it denies players the opportunity to play in finals they deserve to appear in. I was devastated but remembered I had just won one of the biggest derbies in world football.

The excitement grew as I met my family at a bar near my flat. When I arrived around 20 of them cheered and congratulated me. My dad popped open a bottle of champagne and everyone had a drink. At 20, I had played in a legendary derby game, performed well and, most importantly, we had won. A moment to cherish and savour forever. Most of my friends and family had to leave to fly back to London but some stayed overnight. Either way, they had been there to see it and had loved every minute of it. To round off an amazing day, eight of us went out for a meal where we dissected the match in fine detail over dinner before Jess and I headed back to my flat. It was only 10pm but tiredness hit me like a ton of bricks and as I lay on my bed I just drifted off into a deep sleep.

My suspension denied me the opportunity to play in the final which would have been another amazing experience. Just as our victory over Celtic had huge symbolism for Rangers so it was for Hibs, whose fans sang a spine-tingling, scarves aloft, rendition of The Proclaimers' *Sunshine on Leith*. Sadly, the culmination of the game portrayed a less wholesome side to the rivalry as their fans invaded the pitch to goad our supporters and one or two of our players had punches aimed at them which meant we had to get off the pitch pronto.

It wasn't the day we had hoped for but my season at Rangers had been one to remember culminating with that remarkable three-week run in which we lifted two trophies and beat our arch-rivals Celtic.

Those memories will stay with me forever. When Rangers won the SPL title in 2021, I received lots of kind messages from their fans thanking me for my part in the club's recovery. As players, we should always remember that we are only ever passing through. The clubs we play for will always belong, symbolically at least, to the fans.

It was time to head back home for the summer, relax and get ready for another season at Spurs or a return north of the border with Rangers. Maybe.

CHAPTER 13

LEARNING TO MANAGE

My move to Rangers is an example of a loan working out for both parties. I gained invaluable experience and the club benefited from having not just myself but a couple of other young players on loan from English Premier League clubs. Sometimes these moves work, sometimes they don't.

During my season in Glasgow a good friend I'd initially met while playing for Northern Ireland, Jamie Sendles-White, moved in with me during the first half of my remarkable season there, just as Beau would do later in the season, although more for company and a change of scenery. He was able to work from our flat and watch me play most weekends.

Quite randomly, I had helped Jamie secure a loan move to SPL new boys Hamilton Academicals. Jamie had just been released by QPR so while having a coffee with John Brannagan one day I mentioned my mate who was out of contract and looking for a club. Within a couple of hours, John, who knew just about everyone in Glasgow, had called an agent friend who sorted him out with a trial at Hamilton Academicals.

Jamie flew up a few days later for his trial which proved successful and he signed a contract with Hamilton for the remainder of the season, which is why he stayed in my apartment. I didn't like living on my own, so this was the perfect solution.

Hamilton had just been promoted into the SPL but being a small club they had limited finances and played most of their games in front of small crowds in comparison to many larger SPL clubs. Their ground, New Douglas Park, held just 6,000 fans and was barely half full for most matches.

With Rangers still out of the Premiership, only Celtic, Aberdeen and the Edinburgh clubs, Hearts and Hibernian, were able to attract more than 10,000 spectators to their games on a regular basis. To emphasise the gulf between the have and have nots, Celtic and Rangers usually get a whopping 50,000 or more fans to their home games, creating a yawning financial chasm as well as the obvious vocal support.

Neither Jamie nor I were earning a fortune so were hardly living the high life. We'd both lived at home with our parents until now and while we couldn't wait to experience a taste of independence by sharing a flat together, rather than go out we spent most of our Saturday evenings eating a takeaway and watching TV.

However, having played some first team games his contract was suddenly quashed after a disastrous game against Dundee midway through the season. Jamie was hauled off at half time by Hamilton's player-manager Martin Canning who decided to release him shortly afterwards.

Now, you could say young people in any profession are prone to making mistakes and need to be given time to learn – but football just isn't like that. Status, jobs and finances are at stake if the first team performs badly. You could argue Jamie needed support from his manager, but we all know about managerial casualties too. Time is not on their side. Most managers last less than 18 months in their posts so don't have time to develop young players at the expense of delivering the expected results. It was easier for Hamilton to rip up Jamie's contract and start again with someone else.

Ironically Jamie got another chance later in the season by securing a further short-term contract at Swindon Town, where Loz had moved on a season long loan from Liverpool.

Like many other lower league clubs, Swindon chose to bolster their squad with young players signed on loan from Premier League clubs, Lawrence being one of them. He was their regular first team goalkeeper which meant he got bags of experience despite Swindon having three different managers that season which might have led to a change of goalkeeper.

As mentioned, loan moves for young players can be unpredictable. You must go in, knuckle down, hope to learn and add something to the team otherwise you risk being sidelined or sent back to your parent club.

Just to show how unpredictable loan moves can be, that season, Alex Davey, who I have mentioned earlier had been in our team at Pegasus and in Chelsea's academy and was now on a professional contract with them, secured a loan move to Peterborough having done reasonably well at Scunthorpe the previous season.

The see-saw world of football meant Peterborough changed manager early in the season – and although the incoming manager was so instantly impressed with Alex he decided to extend his loan to the whole season - he then changed his mind which left Alex returning to Chelsea midway through the season and under new loan move legislation brought in by the FA, unable to play for anyone else for the remainder of the season, not even his parent club.

This sort of thing means it is even more important for players to get their heads down and work as hard as possible. However, at Swindon, Loz, an outgoing, often cheeky, character who likes to test the water with an occasional laugh, managed to get himself into trouble early in the season which nearly scuppered the value of his move there.

After turning up late for training, Loz was handed a £50 fine and dropped for the next game. He contested it on the grounds he'd had toothache so had arranged an urgent dentist appointment that ran over. Yes, he should have contacted the club to let them know but felt a ticking off was enough and a fine was unfair.

There's an unwritten rule in professional football that it doesn't matter whether you feel it is right or not, if you're fined, you pay up. End of. The money usually goes towards an end of season party or similar anyway, so stays within the group.

Eventually Loz agreed to pay his fine but was so incensed after training he went straight to the bank and asked for £50 in the smallest possible change available. He walked in on matchday with a big grin and bags containing £20 in pennies, £20 in tuppences and £10 in five pence coins.

It was meant to be a joke with no ill will intended. Loz even withdrew the coins and paid the fine properly in notes, giving the coins to his younger brother to slot into charity boxes at a local supermarket.

However, news spread fast and was circulated around player WhatsApp groups. By Monday it was in the press with requests for Loz to do media interviews. The joke rebounded as Swindon sent Loz straight back to Liverpool, who were also furious with him. After a day training on his own at Liverpool, on Tuesday evening Loz swallowed his pride and drove up to Doncaster to watch his Swindon teammates play, just to show his face and to support his colleagues.

It was duly noted and greatly appreciated by Swindon manager Mark Cooper, who offered Loz the opportunity to return immediately to Swindon the following day as they hadn't had time to cancel his loan contract. He was back in goal the following Saturday and remained their first team choice 'keeper for the remainder of the season, playing 36 matches.

With interest from other clubs, Swindon moved speedily to sign Loz on a permanent basis at the end of the 2015-16 season which brought his two-season spell at Liverpool to a close. His £50 fine aside, he'd done alright -- a season long loan that worked.

He was joined by Jamie Sendles-White who, following his experience at Hamilton, had done so well on a short-term contract at Swindon he too was offered a one-year deal for the following season. Sadly, Jamie got a bad knee injury early in the season so missed the rest of the season. After his contract expired, Swindon just couldn't afford to offer an extension to an injured player to see out his recuperation. It was so sad to see this happen to a good friend who had to rebuild his career in non-League football with Leyton Orient the following season, two leagues lower than the level he'd been playing at Swindon.

This is what I mean by saying all kinds of unforeseen factors can affect the future of young footballers. Injury is surely the cruellest. Many people face occupational hazards of one description or another but unless your work involves manual labour the chance of injury is usually slim.

In sport, every day in training and competition carries risk. Often this is little more than a minor niggle, ache or strain that can keep you out for short periods, but longer, more serious injuries are career threatening and can occur at any moment. All your carefully laid plans can come crashing down in an instant and while it is okay for people to assume you should simply dust yourself down and start all over again, imagine for a moment the anguish you can feel if you have been chasing your dream since you were a pre-teen child only to see it removed by circumstances beyond your control.

That is how injury feels for all footballers, not just the boys featured in this book. Sure, 'it's all in the game' as the song goes and players can manage their own on field risk to some extent by pulling out of tackles or aerial duels, but you're in the wrong game if you think you can avoid collisions for too long. Full blooded commitment is the demand. Without it, the game wouldn't be the enthralling spectacle it is.

Among the boys featured in this book both Jack and Mason suffered most from injuries.

Having returned from Gibraltar but failing to find a club back home, Jack went out there again, then joined a spate of non-League clubs, firstly Hemel Hempstead Town, then Chesham United, and later Aylesbury United, who ironically shared Chesham's ground.

He also got a part time job outside the game working for Tesco where his girlfriend worked. Ironic really, because at Watford if someone didn't pull their weight in training or didn't play well enough, our coaches warned us we'd end up stacking shelves in a supermarket. It was the ultimate put down which I now understand to be unnecessarily demeaning. Again, it is a typical blinkered attitude in football to see the world so black and white – professional football on one side, dead end jobs on the other with a huge void in between.

Try as he might, Jack just hadn't made it in football and his career had gone on a similar downward spiral to Mason's. Both had been hit hard by injuries as teenagers and subsequently struggled with the consequences. Football didn't –

couldn't – pay the bills so working in a supermarket provided an income. No shame in that.

Mason was also finding the real world tough. The company that he and his dad worked for needed to cut costs and Mason, being the most recent recruit, was the first to go. Out of the blue, a friend of ours, Jack Waldren, suggested an opening at the hospital where he worked in administration. It wasn't what Mason wanted for a career, but it was a job and shortly afterwards Spenno joined them in his first full time job outside football too, having previously done bits and bobs working with his brothers and his dad.

Spenno meanwhile was playing well at Harrow Borough and scored seven goals in 34 league games from midfield. His first two years after leaving Stevenage had been tough but he was settled, building momentum and gaining confidence.

Matt was settling down to by balancing his time between coaching and playing part-time non-League football.

CHAPTER 14

ON THE ROAD AGAIN

Having had such a good season at Rangers I was more excited than ever to get stuck into pre-season training at Spurs for the start of the 2016-17 season.

I went back to train among the first team squad just as I had the previous pre-season, so I knew exactly how tough it was going to be and, as ever, began in good shape.

Under Mauricio Pochettino, sports science and detailed preparation and training had moved up a notch to get our minds and bodies ready for the forthcoming season.

It is such a world away from British football's dark ages of, sadly, not that long ago when pre-season training consisted of little more than hard-running and fierce training, ostensibly designed to get everyone as fit as possible as fast as possible but so intense the rigours all too often led to players carrying aches and strains into the new campaign that only got worse as the season progressed. Thankfully, the game now has a more scientific and methodical approach with our generation of players able to reap the benefits.

Here's how it went. Our first two days back consisted of tests and assessments. Day one began with a fitness test to assess our maximum heart rate (MHR) followed by sprint and agility tests in five, ten and 20 metre sprints monitored on recording devices.

Next was a V02 max test, undertaken on a treadmill and wearing a mask connected to a machine that collects and measures the volume of oxygen you inhale and exhale with a heart rate monitor to measure our maximum oxygen uptake during different intensities of exercise. To collate this information, we were required to run for about 25 minutes with speed increases every four minutes. During breaks, blood was taken from our finger to test the speed it took for our bodies to produce lactic acid. Before leaving we had to do as many press-ups, pull ups and sit ups as possible in a specific time. All this data was used by our sports scientists to individualise our training programmes.

To round off the day we spent a good hour or so in the pool area – 15-20 minutes going through dynamic stretches, a further 15-20 minutes in hot and cold baths which are like mini pools. Standing in the hot bath after a 15-minute cold bath was definitely the best part of the day.

Day two didn't involve any physical tests but was designed to challenge us mentally, starting with a questionnaire on our basic health with the club doctor, then over to the physio's office for a 30-minute mind test to help us if we were unfortunate to be concussed.

If any of us sustained a head injury during the season, we wouldn't be allowed to restart training until the results matched those we gave in our tests at the start of the season. This was followed by body fat, eye and blood tests.

After lunch, it was back to the physio to check that our joints and muscles were functioning correctly with tests involving movement, flexibility, reaction and jump tests. When these were done, we prepared for the first proper day of pre-season training.

Each day consisted of three main sessions.

In the morning we had to be in the gym for 9am sharp. With so many cameras scattered around the gym to observe us it felt more like a movie set than a fitness centre. After a brief stretch, we did circuit training with each exercise designed to push you to the maximum. The whole team had to replace their kit having lost about two or three kilos in sweat. Training included pull ups, press ups, boxing, resisted sprints and squats.

We were given 30 minutes to recover before heading to the pitch outside. The morning session lasted about 90 minutes and although every drill involved ball work, the emphasis was on the running and fitness rather that the quality of football. Players made routine mistakes as they tired, and we were pushed to go past our physical capability.

The afternoon sessions began at 3pm, allowing us time to have lunch, put our feet up and prepare for the hardest part of the day. We were divided into groups based on our test results. I had made it into the fittest group which meant we did the hardest running and after completing a full set of 'Gacons'– interval training designed by Professor Georges Gacon, the French national middle-distance team manager from 1984 to 1994 and fitness trainer at Marseille FC – we were left gasping for air with the physical challenge of trying to make each set on time pushing every player mentally too.

A month's worth of training, eating and sleeping left me excited for the 24-hour plane journey to Australia for a pre-season tournament. After my successful season at Rangers, I hoped Spurs might offer a long-term contract and my agent pushed them throughout the summer. I wasn't a reserve team or academy player anymore, so I needed to impress Pochettino, the first team coach.

As I got ready to travel to Australia, Spenno finalised a move from Harrow Borough to Hendon. He'd been the main man at Harrow scoring goals from midfield so looked forward to challenge himself at a higher level.

With Mason, Beau and now Jack having hung up their boots, Spenno still hoped to make his way back up the leagues. Coming through an academy isn't the only way to make it. There are Premier League players like Jamie Vardy who came through non-League football. Spenno could still dream of reaching the Premier League via a different route to the rest of us.

Lawrence completed a permanent move to Swindon from Liverpool following his successful season on loan.

Beau spent the summer planning a year travelling overseas and had booked a one-way ticket to Australia. It was ironic to think, having shared a flat together in Glasgow, we'd both now be heading to Australia for different reasons just a few months apart.

I flew out with Tottenham for our pre-season tour to compete in the International Champions Cup in Australia. Jet lag hit me hard as we were only there for a week so there was no point trying to adjust. My body clock wouldn't allow me to sleep until 7am every morning so I took any chance I could to nap during the day. All day I tried to sleep. Training was pointless but the trip was more about games against Juventus and Atletico Madrid than practice.

I made the starting line-up for our first game against Juventus. One good game here could earn a first team contract and put me in a great position to achieve my long-term Premier League ambition. I played in defence against Paulo Dybala, an Argentinian forward who was one of the best strikers in the world.

Still feeling half asleep, I smashed three shots of caffeine down before the game at the famous Melbourne Cricket Ground (MCG) that holds 100,000. It was only a quarter full but the game was shown live on TV so everyone back home could watch. The game was surprisingly quick for a pre-season match and 10 minutes in, the ball broke to me just inside my own half. Roberto Pereyra, another Argentinian international, closed me down and I should have let the ball roll across my body and play it back to our 'keeper but wary of the need to impress I attempted a Cruyff turn which went wrong and the ball bobbled over my foot to put Pereyra through on goal. He passed to Dybala for a simple tap in.

The rest of the half got worse. My body stiffened and I tried too hard so had a torrid time. Pochettino swapped me and the other centre back at half time to different sides of the pitch to see if it would help. It didn't. I was substituted 15 minutes into the second half and had ruined my chance of regular first team football in the opening 60 minutes of the season.

On return to England, I was summoned into Pochettino's office and told I didn't feature in his immediate plans so would no longer train with the first team and was free to leave the club. My time at Spurs, where I had spent the last six years, was over.

I still had another year on my contract so had the option to stay but go out on loan or leave straight away. They offered to find a club if needed and had already had a few offers for me.

MK Dons and Gillingham were interested but my preference was to rejoin Rangers. I spoke to Mark Warburton who confirmed he would like me to return and asked me to leave it with him for a few days. While holding out for an offer from Rangers, my agent spoke to other clubs as I trained with Spurs reserves.

The news wasn't great. MK Dons hadn't been able to wait and had signed someone else in my position. Gillingham didn't make an offer despite their apparent interest either. Rangers wanted to sign me, which sounded great, but offered what we considered to be a weak contract and couldn't guarantee game time as they had brought in other players like Joey Barton, Clint Hill and Jordan Rossiter during the summer who could all play in my preferred position.

I was in a quandary – return to Rangers and risk sitting on the bench for the whole season or hope the final week of the transfer window would offer an alternative. It was a tough call, but I just didn't feel Rangers was quite the right club at that time.

Another option materialised. I was at a Sunday family barbecue to celebrate my godson's second birthday when my agent called to let me know that Rotherham United, who were in the Championship at the time and whose new manager, Alan Stubbs, had managed Hibernian to Scottish Cup victory just a few months earlier, had been in touch. He offered a three-year contract which would triple my wages and, better still, wanted me there straight away. I could have haggled for a better deal but was happy to sign as it seemed such a good opportunity.

I trained with Spurs a few more times while they agreed a transfer fee and drove up to Yorkshire to sign for Rotherham on Thursday, trained with them on Friday, then made my debut at league favourites Aston Villa on Saturday. Quite a whirlwind.

I said goodbye to everyone at Spurs first, not least the coaches who had been so influential to my career. Most of my youth team mates had already left the club, with only Harry Winks who I have stayed in touch with, still there. A new chapter in my football career was about to begin.

From Winning Teams to Broken Dreams

As a young, skinny centre-half competing against some absolute units playing upfront for opposing teams, I struggled to adapt to the physicality of the Championship in the first few games I played for Rotherham. Some of these strikers were Premier League quality whose teams had been relegated. I had to stand up, adapt quickly or fail.

Academies produce players for their own first team. They imitate whatever style of football the first team plays. The head coach usually sets a pattern of play to run through the whole club and the academy follows suit. Sometimes this is based on the values of the club and the football philosophy of its coaching team. There's no point the first team playing nice football if the young players coming through play a more direct style. They won't fit in as there is no correlation between the academy and the senior team.

I had been warned that Rotherham were known to be a proper 'men's club.' By that, they meant their approach to the game was no nonsense, based on working hard, showing fight and competing ferociously. This was different to what I had known as an academy player and professional player at Spurs.

To adapt, I had to learn fast. I did okay to start at first despite the team struggling. As a centre back at Spurs, when our 'keeper had the ball, I was encouraged to slip to the edge of our penalty area and make myself available to receive the ball so we could keep control, commit an opposing player then find a spare man to play the ball forward. If I got this wrong, the other team were straight in on goal but the rewards of breaking through the opposition's top line outweighed the risk of losing the ball.

At Rotherham, when our goalkeeper got the ball, I was expected to sprint up the pitch so he could hoof it up field. My game consequently was less about what I did on the ball and more about tackles, clearances and headers than passing or intercepting.

At Spurs, while we worked on these facets occasionally, our focus was on movement and technical ability. Like other teams in the Championship, Rotherham sought to get the ball into the other team's half quickly or clear it into the metaphorical Row Z – with less care about where the ball went as long as it was cleared from goal.

I played ten games before Alan Stubbs was sacked in double quick time. We had only picked up five or six points in those games so were struggling at the

132

foot of the table. The run up to Christmas was a big test. An experienced Championship manager, Kenny Jackett, replaced Stubbs and I was dropped for his first game in charge. I wasn't even on the bench. After a week's training, I spoke to Jackett and prepared a little speech I hoped would persuade him to put me back in the team.

He'd arrived with a simple strategy. Play as many experienced players as possible and focus on the basics. I didn't fit into his initial plans but after our conversation I like to think he was impressed with how well I had spoken. I was back on the bench for the following game, then started the next match against Leeds United.

Although Leeds proved too strong for us and we lost 2-1, we put in a spirited performance and there were signs of optimism. Sadly, these were quickly snuffed out when Jackett suddenly quit. According to local newspapers, he'd discovered he wasn't going to receive the budget he had expected to improve the team in the January transfer window so left after five games as he felt he couldn't do the job without the required funds.

At first, I thought he had quit too easily but none of us knew the full facts. He was an experienced manager who knew the game inside out and wouldn't have taken the job if he didn't think he could make a difference so must have had good reason to resign so swiftly clearly feeling his reputation, which he had worked hard to cultivate over many years, would be tarnished if he couldn't turn things around.

It left us fearing we had little chance of avoiding relegation. A group of us, called the Costa crew because that's where we met after training, heard the news of Kenny's departure over our coffees. Shocked and saddened, we stayed there all afternoon before going for dinner, with a few of us deciding to drown our sorrows over in Sheffield city centre's Monday student night. The next morning, we struggled with inevitable hangovers in training. Without a manager, we were losing interest and becoming unprofessional.

Paul Warne, a club coach and popular former player with more than 200 games for Rotherham under his belt, took training and was offered the manager's job for the rest of the season. He is still manager of Rotherham at the time of writing this book in 2022. After the next day's session, we found ourselves perched over more coffee discussing the future with a few of us tempted again by another night out in Sheffield.

We had a free day on Wednesday, so I had a lie in. Having been out for two nights out in a row I was dreading Thursday's training session and began to question what was happening to me. I had always taken pride in my positive attitude and willingness to work and train hard, yet I'd stopped showing these characteristics and my football suffered.

Coming from a top Premier League club like Spurs to a smaller club like Rotherham was always going to be a bit of a culture shock but I wasn't prepared for the negative environment I fell into. Culture matters so much in football. Not in a false highfalutin, highbrow way but as the DNA that runs through the club from the top down from the management, coaches, changing room, onto the training ground and, ultimately, the pitch on matchdays. A vibrant, positive culture enables people to achieve great things. A negative culture rots from the inside. Problems are magnified and apathy can fester.

My teammates joked about our poor form, the lack of facilities at our training ground and how soon we might be relegated. Although we had a new stadium we were a relatively smaller club punching above our weight against Championship clubs with larger squads, higher budgets and bigger fanbases we could ill afford to have a negative mindset.

At first, I tried to maintain my positivity and professionalism to see if I could help turn things around. I was fresh in from the Premier League and an England age-representative player. Maybe I could lead and inspire?

I soon discovered such bounciness excluded me from the camaraderie of my teammates which made it harder to build relationships. I was probably seen as a fastidious former academy kid who didn't join in the jokes. I often forced a smile in response, so I didn't look like a killjoy but inside it hurt.

Constant negativity is pervasive. Within a few months I was as guilty as anyone else of gallows humour – always finding something to moan about. It is far easier to be negative than positive to fit in and be one of the lads, and that was how it was at Rotherham back then. If you said something upbeat, the lads battered you. I became the sort of person I'd never wanted to be – a poisonous influence and harbinger of doom in and around the training ground.

Living away from home, I seized on opportunities to go on the town too readily with the lads and did the opposite to what we were told to do by our coaches.

This seemed to happen gradually but, looking back, the scary thing is how quickly this mindset developed. By the time I realised what had happened it was too late.

In January 2017 Warne was given the manager's job until the end of the season. I only played one game under him before my place was taken by experienced defenders who had been at the club for longer. I didn't even make the bench and had descended to fourth choice centre-back. Drifting in and out of the team this way scrambled my head and affected my confidence.

This was the real world of football - managers being sacked, new ones coming in with different philosophies and patterns of play, players shipped in and out in a desperate (and at Rotherham that season, forlorn) attempt to find the right balance to stem the defeats. I struggled to keep up and just six months into my three-year contract I realised I'd made the wrong move and needed to go on loan elsewhere to regain my form.

Peterborough United provided that opportunity. A good League One club pushing for promotion but a level below Rotherham (well, for a few months at least), this seemed an ideal move. In Darragh MacAnthony they had a charismatic, often outspoken, chairman and their young, ambitious manager Grant McCann was in his first job.

I waved au revoir to Rotherham with the aim of returning for the start of the following season as a refreshed and rejuvenated character. Sadly, the plan didn't work. Two months later I was back at Rotherham and due to the terms of my loan move, unable to play again that season.

I started well enough at Peterborough, getting some games under my belt, and enjoying the style of football which seemed to suit my game. After a couple of good performances, we lost the next match, and I was dropped. I didn't think I had put a foot wrong, so met the manager to find out why.

We lost the following game 4-1 at home to Southend, so the change hadn't worked and when I spoke to McCann, he acknowledged he had got it wrong, which was a revelation as managers rarely admit to mistakes. I admired his honesty and thought he was a good coach who made training exciting, structured and relevant. I was back in the side for the following game. Again, we put together a few good results, but I was left out once more.

As soon as we drew or lost, I seemed to be dropped. I went to see him again and we had the same conversation. An apology and promise I'd be back in for the next game without discovering why I had been left out. I had even scored a winning goal in a 2-1 win over Shrewsbury during the three games I'd been back in the team – yet that hadn't been enough to secure my place in the team. Something was wrong and I felt I needed to find out what it was so I could do something about it.

I lost my head when I went to see him this time. It seemed clear to me that I had just been signed as on-loan cover while the club captain was injured. Any chance the manager had to slot him back in, he did. This seemed ridiculous to me – why didn't McCann just pick the best 11 players available?

Maybe I was naive in believing a young on-loan player should have the same privilege as experienced contract players but that was how I saw it as a 21-year-old trying to make his way in the game. Young players strive for consistency and if you're being shunted in and out of a team it is hard to achieve as it is only by playing alongside the same teammates match after match that you build confidence and trust in one another.

The third time this happened McCann pulled me into his office for a meeting. I knew there was every chance I might say something silly but I just couldn't stop myself. McCann wanted to know what my problem was, so I spoke as honestly as possible.

During the conversation I said something truly regretful. I asked McCann why he was picking a team he knew would lose. The moment the words left my lips I knew I'd said the wrong thing. That single sentence sealed my fate for the season and put my entire career in jeopardy.

McCann ordered me to return to Rotherham immediately. I stormed back that was fine by me. It was an angry exchange that did neither of us any credit. A more experienced manager might have laughed it off as the ill-judged comment of a frustrated young player keen to get back into the team having felt he'd been harshly treated. A rocketing and reminder not to say anything like it again might have sufficed.

But there are no excuses for my behaviour. I shouldn't have made such a ludicrous accusation and had no right to question the manager's decision. This wasn't like me but a result of the frustrating circumstances I found myself in. I had been brought up to respect people, to be polite and as helpful and kind to people as possible. I apologised as soon as I could, not just to McCann but other people at Peterborough who I had let down. The football world isn't your average workplace. Things get said in the heat of the moment when passions are high are often better viewed through a long lens.

I was a 21-year-old keen to advance my football career. McCann, in reality, wasn't that much older, in his mid-30s but with a good playing career under his belt and now having to get used to management and no longer able to be one the lads in the dressing room.

I needed to learn from the attitude problem he thought I had – which is why I was in his office in the first place – and learn to control my emotions rather than swan around demanding answers to questions. Equally, I felt he needed to understand how I felt. Right or wrong, there was only going to be one winner. In football, the gaffer's word is final.

I paid a heavy price for that angry outburst. What is it they say about act in haste and repent at leisure? I was unable to play competitive football for the rest of the season. Including the summer months, I didn't play a competitive game for another six months when the new season began with Rotherham relegated as expected to League One. I had plenty of time to contemplate why things had soured for me both at Peterborough and so soon after joining Rotherham.

You can tell from the loans featured in this book just how unpredictable these short-term moves can be. At the end of the day football is a business. Clubs are loyal to their contract players, not just as first teams but as potential future assets they can sell.

While some loan spells result in players moving to the club on a permanent basis, most are designed to enable the player to gain experience. All are shaped to help the club receiving the player to prosper. As a loan player, your interests don't always figure in the equation. You're here today, gone tomorrow, recruited to provide a short-term fillip and hopefully ready to return to your parent club with more experience under your belt or as preparation for the shop window should they seek to sell you.

Without doubt 2016-17 was the worst season of my career with only Spenno and Lawrence doing well among our group that season.

Loz was given a contract extension at Swindon while Spenno's reward for an excellent season at Harrow Borough was a move to Hemel Hempstead Town where, aside from earning more money (on top of his hospital salary), he could train and play closer to home and at the same club Mason and Jack had played at on their way out of football.

CHAPTER 15

HOW LOW CAN YOU GO?

W hile Spenno, Lawrence and I were coping with the anxiety of making our way in professional and semi-pro football in differing ways, maybe we all needed a little of the chilled out life Beau had experienced in Australia.

After 18 months travelling around Australia and New Zealand, he was back home seeking a fresh challenge to replicate the lifestyle he'd been accustomed to Down Under. Whenever we met up, Beau talked endlessly about his travels while we had been trying to keep our careers on track in less exotic towns and cities back home.

We mightn't have been able to walk to the beach every morning or sunbathe after work but were working hard as professional footballers. If we were lucky enough to carve out long and successful careers, we'd have to wait until our mid-30s before we could contemplate emulating the sort of travels Beau had experienced. By then, we'd probably be settled down with kids so had little hope of a responsibility-free, roaming lifestyle.

Beau didn't want to return to the humdrum world of nine-to-five so worked for his dad on his own terms. If he wanted to chill, he did. If he wanted to work over the weekends, he would. He wanted to replicate the carefree lifestyle he had got used to in Australia.

Jack, meanwhile, after two years working at Tesco, wanted to try something new and through a friend was offered a job fitting luxury garden sheds.

At Rotherham, I was now a League One player. Like most players, I had a clause in my contract to automatically reduce my pay by one-third if we were relegated to protect the financial management of the club and cushion the blow of relegation.

I hadn't thought that far ahead when I had signed for them from Spurs the previous season and although it was disappointing, I had always lived within my means so was able to adjust my lifestyle accordingly. Like most young people on good wages, I drove a nice car and enjoyed other trappings of life but always put money aside each month. After a month or two on my new wages, I curbed my spending to match my income.

I was lucky to be able to fall back on my parents' advice, but many footballers lack this sort of support which can be exacerbated by salary fluctuations. If you take on more financial responsibility during good times, you must be able to sustain it during downturns.

The danger is lifestyle creep. The clue is the name. It creeps up on you until you have no idea where your money is going each month. Footballers and other young high wage earners are prone to it. The problem is no one likes to mention it because, well, you know, money is personal, isn't it? That means you tend to suffer in silence on your own. Young footballers have coaches, advisers and mentors they look up to and admire in the game, but financial management role models are thin on the ground. Football also attracts snake oil salesman types who promise high yields on investments only to find it has disappeared years later into some sort of black hole.

Finding someone they can fully trust with the expertise required is difficult, so it is easy to see why so many footballers get ripped off or, conversely, are so understandably cautious they never ask for anyone's advice on money matters. I'm not saying young players shouldn't enjoy the fruits of their labours, and many are more than capable of flashing their cash in all kinds of (sometimes crass) ways, but there needs to be a balance.

Footballers should be able to set themselves up to be financially secure for the rest of their lives but that is only if they can earn consistently and enjoy a long-playing career.

The reality is often far different as you can see from the players featured in this book. So many factors come into play to disturb your plans. The high rate of players who file for bankruptcy because they fall on hard times is an embarrassment to such a cash rich sport.

Wages though were the least of my worries at the start of the 2017-18 season. Fighting for a first team place at Rotherham was a bigger priority. Problem was, I didn't feature in the manager's plans.

As I always had done, I had trained well pre-season but Paul Warne preferred others to play in my position. When I didn't even make the bench for the opening game of the season it was clear I had a choice to either bide my time and wait for an opportunity to arise if someone else got injured or go out on loan again.

On the final day of the transfer window, I was offered a move back to Scotland. A good one, too. Aberdeen had been runners-up in the Scottish Premier League (SPL) for the previous two seasons. Although they didn't compare in size to Rangers, they were a successful and well-respected club. Under Sir Alex Ferguson in the 1980s they had been the last club to break the Auld Firm stranglehold on the SPL, winning three league championships, four Scottish Cups, one League Cup and, most notably of all, lifting the European Cup Winners Cup in 1983.

The city may have been British football's most northern outpost, but Aberdeen was no forgotten backwater. The city has an unreal cosmopolitan boomtown feel fuelled, if you excuse the pun, by the North Sea gas and oil industry.

I was full of optimism as I made the 500-mile journey north. Soon none of these things meant a jot as things went wrong from the very beginning. My first couple of games were a disaster. Like my first loan at Cambridge United, I lost the trust of the manager, Derek McInnes, in the opening weeks and it took several months to get a sniff of further first team action.

It shattered my confidence and the next four months were the hardest of my life let alone my career. I wouldn't say I was depressed because that is a serious diagnosed medical condition, but I was deeply unhappy and turned in on myself. I never thought being a professional footballer, playing the sport I love so much, could make me feel that way.

On one hand I was fortunate to earn good money playing football every day. On the other, I had no friends or family around me so felt lonely and isolated. For some reason, and I can't really explain why, I was reluctant to mix and make friends. I rushed home from training and spent the rest of the day either on my PlayStation or in bed with the curtains drawn. I even convinced myself I was ill at times and ate junk food I knew was bad for me. Once again, as at Spurs a few years earlier, I began over training and punishing my body with tough and unnecessary sessions I didn't need.

My mind was all over the place because I convinced myself I was doing the right thing, failing then beating myself up about everything, overthinking and hating every minute of my existence. I was bored too. Bored with football, bored with life and sad because I was ruining my own career and could feel it slipping through my fingers.

I had let it get so far into my head I was actively preventing myself from progressing and enjoying the thing I loved most and had worked so hard to achieve as a boy from the time I first played in the back garden, through to the enjoyment of junior footy with my mates at Pegasus, our imaginary World Cup school game, progressing just fine at the Harefield academy, not to mention getting over the disappointment of not being offered a scholarship by Watford but earning a dream move to Spurs, being selected for England at under 19 and under 20 level and my amazing on-loan season at Rangers.

I had hit the buffers for the fourth time in rapid succession — released by Tottenham, a dreadful initial spell with Rotherham, brief unhappy loan period at Peterborough, back to Rotherham, where I was unwanted, and now unable to break into the Aberdeen team.

Those first six months at Aberdeen were a self-inflicted cocktail of loneliness, fatigue, boredom and feeling of failure which whisked together to form a recipe for disaster. Young footballers often feel uncertain. Sharing is difficult too. Your teammates, by necessity, are vying for a place in the starting line-up at their club the same as you. True, you have money in your pocket, sometimes, but it can be a lonely experience living in a city where you don't really know anyone and there is no-one to share or do things with, whether it is going for a meal, to the cinema, karting, whatever. I was lost – but not the only one of our group with problems.

Lawrence was playing under a new manager at Swindon, David Flitcroft, who came in with different views to his predecessor, Luke Williams. Loz didn't feature in his plans so rather than sit on the bench, he proactively pushed for a loan move elsewhere. Swindon chairman Lee Power provided that chance. He'd recently acquired Republic of Ireland club Waterford FC and offered Loz the chance to move there for the rest of the season.

Although it wasn't quite the standard he wanted, it worked out to be a great move as Waterford, who'd been recently promoted to the Irish Premier League, challenged for the title and finished fourth, playing in front of gates of around 2-3,000 which is good for Irish football in a wonderful, friendly city. Loz even travelled over with a fellow English player, Courtney Duffus, who was on loan from Oldham Athletic and shared the same agent. He was also able to travel home for a week at a time to be with his family.

By Christmas, I reached the lowest ebb of my career and was ready to give up. I couldn't see a silver lining or figure out how to turn things around. I had always been a positive, confident person with bundles of self-belief. One of my coaches had once described me as a raving optimist which I took as a compliment. That upbeat attitude had all but disappeared now. I had seen this happen to other players, even some of my closest mates, and knew it could spell the end of my professional career.

Three of our group had quit football. Three of us still clung on at one level or another. None of us had made a Premier League start or looked likely to do so. Seven years on from that barbecue in our garden when the future looked bright for all of us the dream was fading fast. Our collective love for the game was wilting and our careers evaporating.

I had a big decision to make. Having made just five appearances in the first half of the season and Aberdeen looking likely to bring other players in during the January transfer window, I had to decide whether to stick it out or return to Rotherham with my tail between my legs.

If I went back to Rotherham, there was every chance I'd find myself stuck in the reserves going nowhere. If I stayed at Aberdeen, I'd be on my own but might get the chance to play a few games if there were some injuries. Aberdeen also had a winter-break training trip to Dubai lined up, so I made the best decision of my career by staying with them. In much warmer weather, we trained well every day, sunbathed and I spent a few afternoons browsing the Emirates Mall with my teammates.

It lightened the mood, but once back in Aberdeen, I returned to my old habit of lying in bed after training to watch Netflix. I was just about to put some dinner on one evening when my brother, Matt, rang. We messaged each other most days so I knew it must be important. I didn't want to pick it up at first for fear of bad news and I wasn't in the mood for a long conversation about football. Just before the call went to voicemail, I decided to pick it up. I hoped it would be a brief chat and it started as normal, very polite with each of us asking how we were doing.

Suddenly Matt's tone changed and became more serious. 'Here we go,' I thought. 'A bollocking from my brother. Just what I need'.

'Dom, you're playing football for a living, you're earning good money and you spend every day kicking a ball about'. Here we go.

By now Matt had moved into IT recruitment and the 'real world' of work, commuting to London at 7am and getting home at 7pm, Monday to Friday. It was a long way from being a full-time professional sportsman and that was the message Matt wanted me to hear. Enjoy it because if you don't, you risk ending up doing what I'm doing. Then you'll be really unhappy.

'Stop overthinking everything, stop worrying about everything. Get rid of your psychologist. Stop going to the gym so often. Stop doing extras after training. Stop writing down your daily plans. Just go out there and enjoy playing football. What you're doing isn't working. It's making things worse. Football is supposed to be fun. It's why you started playing the game so do whatever it takes to get back to that'.

Wow. It hit me like a ton of bricks. I had heard this sort of thing from people before. Some of the lads I had played with and a few coaches had recognised my intensity, but nothing hit home like my brother telling me straight.

It wasn't just what he'd said but the way he said it and when. He told me while I was struggling, not when I was doing well.

I thought hard. I'd forgotten why I enjoyed playing football, the reasons I deeply loved the game so much and the thrills and spills it provided. Many a time in the previous six years I loved football but too many times I also found it a chore and felt the pressure cranking tighter on me.

I'd always considered hard work to be the eternal answer. The harder I tried, the luckier I got. That's the cliché, isn't it? How do you reach Carnegie Hall? Practice. But sheer hard work doesn't always achieve results. If it was as simple as that, we'd all be top professional footballers or masters of any other chosen profession. All those months I flogged myself to death I just hurt myself. It didn't make me faster or stronger and certainly didn't make me a more skilful player. Yet when I should have put some quality time in, I went through the motions.

Matt had seen me struggle. He had watched me perform below my potential and seen me carry the yoke of fear onto the pitch constantly. He knew I needed to lighten the load. Like a true brother, he shouldered the responsibility to tell me straight – and this time I heard the message loud and clear. I had tried absolutely everything over the past 18 months to get my career back on track but one thing I hadn't tried was not trying quite so much. Why not ease back and enjoy it? How simple is that? Why not give *that* a go?

For years I'd had it my own way. All through all my time in academy football as a child and teenager and then at senior, professional level I'd insisted on intensity and always being prepared to work harder than anyone else. Living, breathing, sleeping and eating football. Anxious, keen and eager.

At times, as I have described in this book, I was unafraid to storm into a manager's office and demand my place in the team – regardless of the form of other players. Prepared to disrupt a 10 match winning streak at Rangers (thankfully Mark Warburton had laughed that one off), and again at Cambridge United, Rotherham and, worst of all at Peterborough where, heavens above, I'd even told an experienced, much admired and fully committed former pro and young manager like Grant McCann, he'd picked a team to lose when, in reality, deep down, I was wounded because he'd dropped me from the team.

Always a polite person, well raised by loving parents who had instilled the best values of kindness and generosity of spirit into myself and my brothers, I'd somehow forgotten my manners and been too stubborn to listen to people I could learn from, people who wanted the best, not just for the team, not for themselves, but for me too.

When people talk at differing wavelengths, they call it the dialogue of the deaf. I thought I was focusing hard on what was needed of me, but too often I was just doing my own thing. I could have enjoyed myself more. I was a young man with few worries in comparison to others so needed to start living my life and playing football with less stress and more freedom. Dropping your shoulder in football usually means outmanoeuvring someone to dribble or weave your way past them but it can also mean relaxing, breathing deeply, getting into the zone to enjoy the excitement and thrill of football.

On reflection, I realised the last time I had played a game more excited than nervous was for my local team at Welwyn Pegasus when I was 10 years old. Eleven years later my one and only aim was to rekindle the same joy, to rediscover the inner child who'd once fallen so headily in love with football. Reality bit. If I didn't learn to do that now, I wasn't going to be in the game much longer.

My affection had all but evaporated, lost within a mad scramble to jump through hoops, inch ahead of others and knuckle down to become a good pro schooled to mercilessly grind out results and constantly keep proving my worth. Hard work alone couldn't help achieve this anymore. I had to go back to that primal love of football as a fun sport to play. Nothing else mattered more.

An immediate need was to end my loneliness. Born in Inverness where he had played for the local big club, Inverness Caledonian Thistle, before signing for Celtic, Ryan Christie was a teammate who'd also joined Aberdeen on loan that season. He was the same age as me with a similar mentality. He too lived alone in a flat on his own just 100 metres from mine so we decided he would move in as we liked each other's company. Alongside other younger lads at the club we started to go out socially too.

I began to enjoy training, smiling more and even having a laugh with the manager. I still didn't play regular first team football for a couple of months, but I stopped worrying about it. When my chance came in the last five games of the season, after the fixtures split between those clubs in the top half of the SPL table who would compete against each other for the remaining two available Europa League places, I was in the starting line-up and played in all the remaining games, drawing two and winning three including a memorable 1-0 win against champions-elect Celtic at Celtic Park in front of 60,000 supporters on the final day of the season. This secured our runners-up place and a Europa League spot for the following season.

My change in attitude earned more game time. Hardly rocket science and not confined entirely to football, sport or work but to life itself, we enjoy things with a more relaxed attitude.

Ryan Christie, who I had shared a house with and had been a good teammate, went back to Celtic where he started playing regularly and progressed to the Scottish national side. In 2021 he moved to Bournemouth in the English Championship.

Lawrence had made the most of his move to Waterford in the Republic of Ireland to boost his love for football having been in and out at Swindon under different managers and headed back for the final year of his contract. His manager at Waterford, Alan Reynolds, was sensitive to the demands of family life and allowed him to fly home to England after some Friday night games so he could spend a week back home and return ahead of their next game the following weekend.

For a salutary lesson of what we needed to achieve, once again, perhaps slipping quietly under the radar, was the only one of our group who'd had a good season and was looking upwards. Spenno, who'd never lost his love of football and had played almost every game, finished the season as a stand-out player for Hemel Hempstead.

His move had been a good one and he had done more than enough to move up another league if he pushed for it. He was happy at Hemel however and planned to stay for at least another six months.

Beau, Jack and Mason were increasingly accustomed to life outside football and had settled into decent jobs. Importantly, they were happy with their lives and had fully accepted that football hadn't turned out to be the dream they'd hoped when we were 16 and younger.

The rest of us were still just about living the dream. Well, some people may have thought we were. The reality was that it had taken the last five games of the season for me to put a run together at Aberdeen.

I had endured the toughest season of my career but was ready to look forward to a bright future.

CHAPTER 16

SPANISH EYES

I wouldn't want anyone to read this book and feel football was nothing but a trail of misery for the six boys featured.

We had our ups and downs for sure. Some setbacks have been worse than others but they have been interlaced with moments of genuine joy that transcend the experience of most people's lives. One way or another, we all feel proud of what we have achieved.

It may not have been the Premier League or bust journey we had set our hearts on, but we had experienced the trials and tribulations of trying to make it in the most competitive sport in the world in the most competitive country at its most intense time ever.

English football is revered worldwide with the Premier League its jewel in the crown brand. As with most vocations, by our early 20s things had started to fall into place for each of us as the drama of our teenage years slowed down.

We'd set out as six typical elite football academy graduates and were now settling down to a level we each found comfortable. For some, like Beau, the game wasn't ultimately for them. Injury took its toll too, not least for Jack and Mason who quit the game through injury and frustration. Again, no shame. Better to have tried than not.

After leaving the academy system at different stages, we'd had an array of experiences and differing rates of progress. Four of us earned a living from the game, three of us regularly. Along the way we'd won things, been through promotion and relegation, been bought and sold and experienced many of the highs and lows you get in football. We had a lot to feel proud of, individually and collectively.

Some memories are just plain 'you had to be there' moments.

Take the summer of 2018 for instance, when I went to Madrid for a summer holiday with Jamie Sendles-White, mentioned earlier in this book, and Danny Rogers, a good friend I had made at Aberdeen.

Just four days into our holiday, considering Jamie and Danny hadn't met before, they were getting along like a house on fire. Too well in fact. Both were extraverts so getting a word in proved difficult.

We sat in an Irish pub waiting to watch Rotherham United in the League One play-off final at Wembley. Contractually, I was still a Rotherham player but hadn't been part of their 2017-18 team. I had been on loan at Aberdeen so couldn't claim any credit for Rotherham's promotion hunting season, even though I stood to benefit by becoming a Championship player again and my wages – just as they had decreased the previous season when we'd been relegated - would rise again. Fair to say, I had more than a vested interest in the outcome of the game.

That day at Wembley belonged to the lads who had worked hard all season, got themselves into the play-off final and here was I having a beer in Madrid with my mates hoping to benefit from their hard work. It felt strange.

While it was a bit cloudy in Madrid, back home it was the hottest day of the year. Wembley was only a quarter full but with the chance of returning to the Championship at stake the atmosphere reflected the significance of the match.

It was a decent game, but I was nervous and desperate for a result. So much was on the line and the game went to extra time with Rotherham scoring the winner in the last minute. I watched that match as if I had gambled my entire savings on it and, thankfully, the right result came up.

I was ecstatic and we stumbled out of the bar having had a few celebratory drinks. It was situated just a few hundred metres away from the main square and as we came out the place was packed. You literally couldn't move. The road had been closed off and police had erected barriers that left lines of people crammed together on either side of the street as far as the eye could see. As we tried to make our way through the crowd back to our hotel, we suddenly realised what was going on.

All we kept hearing was, 'Hala Madrid, Hala Madrid'. The night before we'd watched the UEFA Champions League final in a small café next to the Bernabeu, Real Madrid's famous stadium. We hadn't been able to find a seat so had stood in the entrance and watched the game through a window. Real had won and were now coming home to lift the trophy in front of their fans. It was an incredible sight. As the coach arrived the place went wild, erupting with screams and whistles. The players walked into the building and made their way up onto the balcony where everyone could see them.

After a long countdown, Sergio Ramos, Real's captain, hoisted the trophy aloft to huge cheers and each player took their turn to lift it too. After seeing Ronaldo, we wandered back to our hotel, and I kept thinking of those players we had just seen with the greatest prize in European football. The club I was with had just been promoted and I was on holiday watching it. What a great day it had been. So many times I had begged for some good luck and it hadn't materialised.

I had turned my life and career around. That call from my brother earlier in 2018 had sparked a wholly fresh approach. There was no point being in football if I wasn't going to enjoy it. Had I continued with the intensity of the previous years I was going to find myself hating the game and exiting it rapidly. Instead, I decided to go with the flow, find joy and happiness in each session and do whatever it took to fall in love with football again. In changing my approach, I was ready to accept if I couldn't rekindle the same enjoyment then I would need to find a different career. Football became secondary to happiness, and it should always have been that way around.

My dream was always to play in the Premier League, a shared ambition for all of our group. At times it had seemed tantalisingly within the grasp of each of us. I had seen three of my friends become so disillusioned and shattered by the experience they had stopped playing football completely and saw many other friends struggle to try to make it in professional football. Our expectation was always to play at the top level. It was the Premier League or nothing.

In time you learn to reset your sights and each of us realised that playing at any level of football is an achievement to be proud of. My life had revolved around this one dream for so long it had taken over my whole existence at the expense of happiness and any sense of a wider vision. Each loan move I made, even the transfer to Rotherham, was all with a singular view in mind. It was an obsession that ate me up and clouded my judgement. It was at the root of many of the mistakes I made.

After that call from my brother, I gave up on dreams, something I'd been told so often never to do. Sure, you must set goals and have targets but you need to live in the moment.

It felt better ditching the endless planning and heaping pressure on myself that had sucked the joy and pleasure out of playing the beautiful game. Worse still, it made me feel like a failure when I was far from that, if only I took time to stand back to appreciate what I had rather than what I hadn't.

Most people would give their eye teeth to be a professional footballer just for one day yet here was I moaning about the fact I wasn't playing at the exact level I had envisaged.

I came to accept there was no point worrying why I wasn't being picked for the first team or why I had just had a bad game as that wasn't going to make me any happier. I'd had all these negative emotions swirling around like a vicious circle and dragging me down.

Then there's control. Things happen in football, as in all aspects of life, for a reason. Mostly, for players, they are out of your control. Sure, you should always strive to do your best but other people (managers and coaches mainly) are paid to make those decisions so there's no point worrying about it. I had to let go. I found I got on better with managers and coaches because I didn't feel the need to challenge them for failing to give me what I wanted rather than what I deserved. I found a beautiful balance between my football and wellbeing, and if I can carry on like that, I hope to have an enjoyable, lengthy career.

Some of the other lads were settling down too.

Matt had grown to love non-League football and everything about it, in particular the close community feel of local clubs and their supporters – the chance to play a match and share a beer with fans in the clubhouse afterwards. For Matt, the professional dream was over, but his love of football was very much still intact although he wanted to get back into the game full time to help and guide footballers.

An unusual move materialised for Lawrence after he was released by Swindon at the end of the 2018-19 season. He was called up to the Chilean national team having been eligible through his dad, who was Chilean, and had good connections in the country. He had become a youth international while at Tottenham, but in 2019 he was called up to the national side as third choice goalkeeper, playing in the same squad as notable players like Alexis Sanchez and Arturo Vidal.

Most of the campaign had been spent travelling to compete in international matches but, domestically, Loz signed for Chilean Premier league club, Everton de Vina del Mar. Sadly his season ended abruptly before he'd had chance to play a game due to anti-government protests which made the country unsafe. Curfews were introduced to curtail street riots. Desperately missing his family back home too, Loz got out of Chile as quickly as possible to end a crazy but memorable experience.

As for me, well, in 2018-19 I returned for a second season on loan at Aberdeen and played 40 matches, more than in any previous season, including a Europa League game against Burnley.

Those two years at Aberdeen had a profound effect on my life. Sure, it was tough at times, but what a fantastic experience it had been to play week in, week out in the Scottish Premiership. I also found I was able to put my energy into other things and found other hobbies to focus on rather than fretting over football 24/7. I learned to appreciate training and playing football more – and discovered that rather than accepting the long-held dogma that you need to concentrate 100 percent on football that you perform better when your downtime is occupied by things.

I also got to play alongside some truly gifted footballers in my time at Aberdeen, not just Ryan Christie who I mentioned in the previous chapter and is now a Scottish international, but players like Kenny McLean, Graeme Shinnie, Scott McKenna and Max Lowe, who are all playing in the English Premier League or Championship and for a highly regarded manager in Derek McInnes.

More importantly I had finally rediscovered my love of the game.

Although I had the option of signing permanently for Aberdeen, I decided it was time to lay down my own roots and find a club closer to home.

CHAPTER 17

FOR SPENNO'S SAKE

O n a warm Tuesday evening in May 2019 all six of our group headed down to Vicarage Road, the home of Watford FC. The season had ended a week earlier and we were all back home from wherever we had spent the season.

We had to be at the stadium for 5.45pm, to allow sufficient time for those lads who worked day jobs to negotiate the rush hour traffic. It was the first time since the barbecue two years earlier when none of us had fancied a kickabout that we'd all been together.

Not tonight though. Most of us were 23 now (although Loz was a year older), none of us had played in the Premier League but at least tonight we could say we'd played on a Premier League pitch together.

Spenno, who had organised the evening, welcomed us at the gate, escorting each of us towards the visitors' changing room past the pitch and up the tunnel. People were starting to fill the stands for a charity match Spenno had arranged between Hemel Hempstead Town and Wingate & Finchley – the two clubs where he had spent most of his time.

It was ten years since I last played at Vicarage Road for Watford's academy and things had changed. The old main stand, called the Elton John Stand in recognition of the legendary singer-songwriter's contribution as chairman in the 1970s and 80s, had been rebuilt. The away dressing room was allocated to Wingate for the night. The kitman had hung our shirts numbered one to 18 on the pegs and our starting line-up was pinned to the tactics board.

A sucker for punctuality I was first to arrive. Sadly, as I was about to sign for Queens Park Rangers having just finished my second season at Aberdeen, I couldn't risk playing in case I picked up an injury which might scupper the deal, so I assisted Spenno instead.

Mark Warburton had become manager at QPR. When he asked if I'd like to join them it couldn't have been more perfect. Here was a manager who had known me since I was a young academy player at Watford and had managed me at Rangers. I suited his style of play and, more importantly, I knew he trusted me. I also knew some of the players and coaches there too. I felt it was where I needed to be. My home life was settling down. I had finally moved in with my girlfriend, Jess. We'd been going out for six years and when Jess, who is from Watford, heard I was coming home she found a nice flat for us to rent on the canal in Harefield. Talk about coming full circle.

First of our team to breeze in was Lawrence in his customary confident way. He was about to join Leyton Orient, a team he was still with at the time of writing this book, which was only 20 minutes from where he had grown up. Loz walked straight over to the No.1 jersey as our goalkeeper for the night.

Alex Davey – also mentioned a few times in this book – arrived next and pulled on the No. 4 shirt, just as Jack stepped in. Having hung up his boots ages ago, 'I am not ready for this lads', were his nervy opening words as this was going to be his first game in a long while. We welcomed him with a warm hug, safe in the knowledge that as a versatile player he could fit in anywhere.

After leaving the game to work at Tesco, Jack found a job fitting luxury sheds and had saved some money to buy a flat in Wendover in Buckinghamshire where he'd moved in with his girlfriend. Jack changed careers by taking a three-month intensive course to train as an electrician. Spenno's dad was part of a firm of electricians and had given Jack the nod that a job would be waiting for him if he qualified. It was a big sacrifice to make as he had no income for three months and had to dip into his savings to pay for the course, but with a guaranteed job at the end Jack decided it was worth investing in his own future.

Having had his chance of a football career dashed by a knee injury, it was a long time since Jack had been in these surroundings, and he wasn't sure where we wanted him to play. On the team sheet, Spenno had marked him down as a right sided midfielder.

Just like in our Watford academy days the aim was for Jack to support Beau at right back and he breezed in next with long blond hair cascading down his neck, wearing a cap, shades, baggy white t-shirt, rolled up trousers and flip-flops. Like a scene from a film, Beau whipped off his hat and glasses, ran his fingers through his hair, swished his hair to one side then gave us all a hug.

Yup, that was Beau alright – always aspiring to pull off a cool biker look. 'Uh-oh, here we go' was our usual collective response when we met up with him and we often wound him up for trying just a little too hard to look like an Australian or American dude. Deep down, I guess we were all a tad jealous of how he somehow managed to effortlessly pull off the look he wanted.

Following his travels, Beau had re-joined New Curious Generation, the digital marketing and merchandising agency he had helped get started, which by now had tripled in size, moved to larger offices and diversified its product range. But Beau preferred something more tactile and after becoming a qualified carpenter he set up his own carpentry business called Ashridge Bespoke with a colleague.

Film star good looks or not, tonight Beau had to knuckle down at right back and he was apprehensive having not played football for a couple of years.

Nonchalant as ever Mason was the last to arrive. He also hadn't played for a couple of years but still looked more like a top footballer than the rest of us. We used to wind Mason up by saying he was more concerned with his image than his football, but he played the part well, carrying the kind of swagger strikers need to score goals.

After football, Mason had several different jobs but has become a self-employed qualified electrician used to long days, often leaving his house at 6am to reach a construction site and returning as late as 7.30pm.

He has vowed to get back into football, but those long hours may mitigate against it. Try as you might, it is difficult to put any serious physical effort into football if you are working such long and arduous days. He is also going to continue with his electrician qualifications.

The reality is, like all the boys featured in this book and thousands more across the country, we are utterly consumed by football and obsessed with the aspiration and expectation to play the sport we love. The further you go in the game, the greater chance you seem to have but when it doesn't happen the disappointment is more acute.

As our only recognised striker for the night Mason strode over to claim the No 9 shirt, looking like he had just signed for Man Utd on a five-year contract. He was leading the line against Hemel tonight, no mistake.

You'll have gathered by now we were a few players short for a full 11 aside game and were missing a left back and winger, No.10 and a centre back. Up stepped our mates Alfie Barrett, Jack Waldren, Sam Szmodics and Joe Mistretta, all good friends with our group.

Jack had been in our Watford under 16s team, Sammy, a midfielder, became friends with a few of the lads when they met on holiday and is currently playing for Peterborough United. Joe slipped into the left back berth with Alfie in the centre of defence.

The dressing room was designed in a semi-circle with lockers facing the table at the front of the room and boasted a large shower room with baths, a manager's office, and physio beds. We were able to imagine changing for a proper Premier League matchday.

Spenno had put together quite some team and although we were supposed to be Wingate & Finchley, it felt more like a side that could compete in the Championship. The bench was full of Spenno's former teammates who wouldn't appear until the second of the four quarters we were due to play. The team changed every quarter as some players were only fit enough to last one quarter at a time. The Hemel team comprised a mix of Spenno's family and recent teammates. Although it was a bit of fun, we were determined to win our one and only game together.

Just like any other Premier League team arriving at an away ground, we spent 15 minutes or so checking out the pitch. The main stand was filling up and we each looked out for our friends and family and many more folks we had met on our journey over the past ten years or more.

We all came to support a great cause - Spenno.

Spenno's journey had been different to the rest of us. He'd never played in a Premier League club academy as such but had made up the numbers among the pupils at Harefield and, like Loz, had played college football prior to moving into local semi-pro football.

In spring 2018, towards the end of his first season at Hemel Hempstead Town, Spenno picked up a shin injury but was determined to finish the season as they were pushing for the play-offs in the Southern League Premier Division. Having played a vital role in the team's success all season, he fought through the pain barrier in the hope that a summer rest would help him recuperate. It happens all the time in football.

Hemel's physios thought it was little more than a bruised shin but it troubled Spenno all summer and he constantly tried to ease the pain by placing ice packs on his skin. When pre-season arrived, his shin showed no sign of improvement and he was unable to train with Hemel's mystified physios unable to satisfactorily diagnose his injury.

Finally, Spenno had a scan which revealed a fractured shin bone. He was given crutches, told to stay off his feet for three months, prescribed medication to help heal the bone and advised to ice his leg regularly.

The pain intensified which affected his sleep, causing Spenno to frequently wake up in agony. By Christmas 2018, he could take no more and booked a further, more detailed scan he hoped would get to the bottom of things.

It was catastrophic news. In late January 2019 Spenno was told the devastating news that the shin fracture was actually a seven-centimetre tumour in his tibia bone. Following a biopsy, Spenno was finally diagnosed on February 8, being told he had a rare form of bone cancer – Ewing's Sarcoma. It's such a rare cancer that it accounts for just 0.2 per cent of all cancer cases in the UK, roughly some 600 people a year. It was devastating news but at least explained the pain Spenno was suffering. Following a hastily arranged meeting with an oncologist and surgeon, he discovered it was potentially going to be treatable with chemotherapy and surgery. He began bi-weekly cycles of intense chemotherapy on February 20.

The day he had found out he had cancer, Spenno sent a message to our group. It was heart-breaking to read and none of us knew how to respond. Our best friend, one of the fittest and healthiest guys in our group, had been diagnosed with cancer. I spoke to some of the lads on the phone but spent most of the night staring into space unable to think straight. How had this happened? Why Spenno? How come it had it taken seven months to diagnose? Was he going to be alright?

We were desperate to be provided with further information, but Spenno had to deal with his own emotion first while a plan of action was devised by his doctor. Spenno's chemotherapy began at University College Hospital Macmillan Cancer Centre in Central London with five days of intense treatment across nine cycles until surgery.

Spenno started to lose his hair and it wasn't until after the fifth cycle of chemotherapy that he had enough energy to come out with us for a meal. Even then, if any of the lads had reported the slightest illness he wouldn't have been able to join us as the risk of infection was too great.

It was the first time I had seen Spenno since his treatment and it was a truly emotional experience. He wore a hat to hide his hair loss, looked pale and skinny and needed crutches to move around. When I exchanged an affectionate hug, I sensed how important the evening was for him. Never a touchy-feely sort of guy, the power and depth of those hugs told you all you needed to know. He seemed in good spirits as we reminisced about happier times and could have talked all night. Spenno tired easily though and nodded off a few times because of the medication he was taking. A great night ended with lots more emotional hugs. We didn't know when we might see each other again.

In the previous months his girlfriend, Sarah, had pretty much moved into the family home to care for him full time. He needed constant attention and someone to take him to hospital on a regular basis, so she shared the duties with Spenno's mum, Claire.

When we first discovered the news of Spenno's cancer, the tempting question to ask when you love football as much as we do is whether he would be able to play football again. Then it sunk in. Being cancer free and able to walk again was Spenno's main aim. Football no longer mattered.

After nine cycles of treatment Spenno had to undergo surgery to remove the tumour and some of the surrounding bone. Surgeons removed 15cm from his tibia bone and it was sent to the lab for testing. Great news, Spenno had responded well to the chemotherapy and 95 percent of the cancerous cells were necrotic. Things were looking promising. After a few weeks of bed rest, Spenno underwent another operation to insert a metal rod into his tibia to support the bone to allow him to be more weight bearing on his crutches.

The plan was to use a Ilizarov external frame to grow new bone in the gap in his tibia. First, he had another five rounds of chemotherapy to go through to ensure the cancer wouldn't return. In the meantime, doctors had seen nodules on scans of Spenno's lungs but couldn't determine if these were cancerous as they hadn't changed in shape or size during treatment. His oncologist was certain that as Spencer had responded so well to chemotherapy initially, these wouldn't be an issue even if they were cancerous as they should respond to the final rounds of intense chemotherapy.

After undergoing the final five rounds of chemotherapy, in late September 2019 Spencer was given the provisional news that things were looking good. He was told he wouldn't need any further chemotherapy at this stage and was given to go ahead to see his surgeon regarding the Ilizarov external fixator, to regrow his tibia bone over the next four to five months. When Spencer told us the news, it was the best we'd ever heard. That night we went to Spenno's favourite restaurant, L'artista, and he even had a few glasses of red wine to celebrate.

In October 2019 Spenno began the journey of regrowing his tibia under the care of the Royal Orthopaedic Hospital. This meant another operation to insert the external fixator onto his leg, connected directly through the skin to his tibia bone. He'd then have to go on for the next few months manually turning the screws on the frame daily, enabling the bone to grow as it was stretched by the frame. This was the best possible option for him to begin to walk again as normal in the future.

Unfortunately, just a couple of months into Spenno's bone growth journey, a check-up X-ray at Christmas 2019 raised suspicions when nodules on his lungs appeared larger than they were previously. In January 2020, he had an MRI scan that revealed this was indeed the case and almost exactly a year on from his original diagnosis, he was re-diagnosed with metastatic Ewing's Sarcoma. This confirmed the disease had spread to his lungs.

This was hard news to take. Spenno had to restart his chemotherapy immediately. Different drugs were needed as the first cycle hadn't worked. Which brings us back to Vicarage Road.

As a die-hard Watford fan like the rest of his family, the aim of the night was to attract as many people as possible to watch a game of football at Vicarage Road so the proceeds could support Spenno's family (his mum had stopped working and his girlfriend Sarah also helped out) and raise funds for Cancer Research UK.

Wingate & Finchley v Hemel Hempstead Town was chosen as Spenno had friends at both clubs. As we returned to the dressing room following our walk around the pitch, Spenno came in to run through the plan. The lads put on their boots and pads, then we all walked back on to the pitch with lots of people in the stands who had turned up to support the cause including our families and many of the friends we had made on our different footballing journeys.

It was truly inspirational and emotional to see so many people behind Spenno's fight to beat cancer, including folks we hadn't seen since school and football friends who were gutted not to get the call to play. Sadly, we had limited places. Spenno had even organised a referee and assistants to officiate so it would be a proper game.

The game was competitive. Each quarter lasted 25 minutes and we all knew the first quarter would matter most as that was when the best and fittest players were on the pitch and it was the only part of the evening when we were all going to play together.

Mason put us in front with a tap in from close range. Well, sort of. The ball went wide to Jack who crossed to Mason. He swung his left boot at the ball, missed, and the ball struck the inside of his right ankle and rolled into the left bottom corner. It was so comical none of us could celebrate because we couldn't stop laughing.

Nonetheless, a goal is a goal. We'd taken the lead and played some decent football, passing the ball out neatly from the back. Beau and Joe were overlapping the two Jacks, Westlake and Waldren, with Alfie and Alex solid behind. I just barked out orders as Spenno's sidekick for the evening. More than anything it was good to see the lads playing together as a team for the first time.

We ran out 4-3 winners, even though some of the lads tired and missed easy chances after tripping over their own feet. Spenno had achieved something truly amazing – he had brought so many special people together to support his battle with cancer and the evening was a great success. The best part was seeing Spenno sat in the home manager's dugout watching his best mates battle it out on the hallowed Watford turf he loved so much and had always dreamt of playing on. It was a night all of us will always remember.

Afterwards we showered and made our way to a pub opposite the stadium. Many of those who had watched were already there, waiting for Spenno to arrive. He walked in a proud and content man, if slightly shocked to see so many people come to support him. Hundreds turned up that night to raise money for Spenno.

Unfortunately, as Spenno's treatment continued to not be as successful as we had first thought, he was trying his best to find new treatments and trials. He was so determined to live. In June 2020 he was given the gut-wrenching news that as the second, third and fourth line chemotherapy hadn't worked on the nodules in his lungs. His cancer was now defined as terminal.

Spenno refused to accept this diagnosis. In August 2020 he set off with his girlfriend Sarah to both Germany and Latvia, desperate to try new treatments that were unavailable in the UK. Unfortunately, although the treatments in both countries initially proved to be promising, the cancer fought back stronger than ever. Close to defeat, in October 2020, after feeling like he'd hit the end of the road, Spenno and Sarah took one last gamble, travelling down to Mexico to a clinic that offered innovative treatments that weren't on offer in the UK.

They spent seven months there, with the treatment initially working well, giving Spencer hope again that he might one day be cancer free. This specialised treatment unfortunately came at a high cost and required constant funding. Of course, we all did what we could and managed to raise around £130,000 for Spencer, which extended his life significantly, something that is invaluable.

In the summer of 2021, Spenno came home to the UK, a country emerging from the grip of three Covid 19 lockdowns which has claimed the lives of 160,000 UK citizens at the time of writing this book, to fulfil a dying wish.

On July 11, England reached the final of the European Championships on home soil. It was football mad Spenno's dream to see England lift the trophy. Even though he was desperately ill, we managed to get tickets for Spenno and his brothers for the semi-final and final. Spenno went to England's triumphant semi-final victory over Denmark but was too ill to attend the final. He died a few days later.

Heartbroken doesn't come close to how we all felt – not just for Spenno or for ourselves but for his family and especially for Sarah. You don't expect your friends to lose their lives so early in life and any thoughts we may have had about football seemed trite in comparison.

That said, far away from the fantasy world of the Premier League we dreamt about, at the gritty end of the game, the non-League football family, cherished Spenno's memory around the country. He was – to steal the fans' song lyric – one of their own.

Spenno was indeed one in a million and one of our closest mates too – the most honest and lovely friend you could ever wish to meet who, like fine wine, would have grown better with age.

We all loved him to bits – and carrying his coffin was one of the toughest things I have ever had to do in my life on a day of immense sadness, a time when football didn't matter but friendship and camaraderie counted more.

The next day I had to pull on my boots for QPR's opening game of the season against Millwall.

I know I speak on behalf of all the boys whose collective story is told in this book that we have lost our greatest mate. Although people often say time is a healer, we are still reeling from the consequences and will do for some time yet.

Our immediate thought is to help support research into Ewing's Sarcoma and to support families like Spenno's, who need to provide care when this cruel disease strikes.

That's why the proceeds of this book are going to Sarcoma UK and why I was delighted to accept the role of being an ambassador for this worthy charity and do all that I can to raise its profile.

We miss him beyond belief. Everything each of us achieves from here on in will be in memory of Spenno, be it in or outside of football which, jokingly, the great Bill Shankly once infamously defined as 'not a matter of life or death but more important than that'.

It is hard to appreciate the full irony of that quote until you have lost someone quite so dear as Spencer, someone so madly, keenly, and passionately in love with football.

From Winning Teams to Broken Dreams

EPILOGUE

THAT'S LIFE

A t the end of the match for Spenno, we formed a circle at the bar to recall our favourite moments in football. As the evening wore on and the beer flowed the conversation naturally moved to our career highlights.

We had all started in top level academies and been on our own individual journeys. Beau, Jack and Mason have given up playing completely and fallen out of love with the game but still had many happy memories to look back on. We recalled our school days at Harefield and our individual highlights.

For Jack it was reaching the Milk Cup final and beating Chelsea along the way.

For Beau, although he was first to leave the game out of all of us, he cherishes the opportunity he had to pursue his dream at least partly.

Mason remembered the goals he scored for Spurs at under 16 level – not least a game at Charlton where he scored twice despite turning up in a lurid pink t-shirt and, quite rightly, being endlessly ribbed about it. Best way to silence the banter of your micky taking teammates? Score goals. Works every time.

For Loz, it was the pride in telling his father he'd been called up to the Chilean national team for the first time and getting to train alongside the likes of Sanchez and Vidal.

Finally, Spenno simply enjoyed being able to train with the Watford crest on his chest. On his special night he just hadn't been able to resist touching things with the Watford badge on.

For some, the journey is over. For others, the embers still glow. Either way, football has left an indelible mark on us all. It shaped our lives from a young age and played a hugely significant role in our upbringing. It has been a constant factor in our development from children to teenagers and onto adulthood.

We each had our own burning ambition to reach the top, and vivid aspirations to be the best players we could be. Moreover, it brought us together as a band of brothers.

Looking back at that memorable barbecue day when we were 15, we were all on the same pathway in our football journey. Much has happened since, of course. We have each taken different routes, fought our own battles and faced our own unique trials and tribulations. There has been some joy there too.

We have tried as hard as possible to make our way in the most competitive sport on the planet in a football mad country which has the most high profile league in world football.

We knew we had a collective battle to fight together for Spenno. When needed, I hope we stepped forward and did our best. What we have all realised is that nothing is more precious than life itself. Spenno's ill health put a lot of things into perspective for each of us, I believe.

There is a lot of heartache within the pages of this book. I have tried to explain the difficulties and dilemmas involved in trying to become a professional footballer and express reservations about the process involved and the shortcomings as well as the many benefits of the English football academy system and the progress in the development of young footballers.

Right or wrong, I've tried to tell it as it is, not as someone trying to spin a yarn or forward a particular cause but to tell it from the inside by recounting the experiences of six mates.

No one sums up our indominable spirit more than Loz, whose remarkable rise from obscurity to become a reserve team goalkeeper at Spurs and Liverpool typifies what can be achieved with a positive attitude.

Now safely back home after his South American experience, he is grateful for the security and joy his family have brought to his life. He is currently playing for Leyton Orient in League Two but ever hopeful of returning to keep goal in the Premier League one day. Without doubt, I believe Loz is capable of it.

As for Beau, well, he didn't have the greatest of experiences in football, not least during his last two years in Watford's academy and ultimately lost his love of the game.

But football isn't the be all and end all. It provided us with some of the best days of our lives but also some of the worst. Sometimes it broke our hearts, at other times it gave us hope. We had incredible highs and some horrible lows. Looking back, I sometimes feel we had aspects of childhood stolen from us.

At 21, I realised I hadn't enjoyed playing the game much since I was 10 years old. Was it all worth it? The jury is still out.

We all started playing for the love of the game. We shared dreams of playing in packed stadiums, being seen on TV and winning games. Now the only things we care about are our health and happiness and those we love.

Our group of friends share a special sense of togetherness. When one of us succeeds, we celebrate in unison. If any of us receives bad news, we commiserate together too. Parallel lives, different journeys.

Our collective journey to become professional footballers has never been just about success or failure. It is about enjoying our journey together.

Towards the end of his life Spenno urged us to live in the moment rather than overthink things. There's wisdom in that thought and something we're all determined to do from now on. As ever, ebullient Loz summed it up best: when our time is done, we'll have a great party upstairs in heaven when we are all finally reunited, Spenno included.

Touch wood, there will be lots of time to go until then, of course. We fought to try to help save the life of our friend, Spenno, a fight we ultimately lost but only after we gave it our very best effort.

Just as it always was, we fought it together – and everything we will ever do in our lives will somehow be for Spenno and to live the dream of a full life he sadly never had.

Nothing else matters more.

Dominic Ball

BIOGRAPHIES

Dominic Ball
B Welwyn Garden City DOB: 2 August 1995
Academy: Watford & Tottenham
Professional clubs: Tottenham, Cambridge United (loan) Rangers (loan), Rotherham United, Peterborough (loan), Aberdeen (loan)
Current club: Queens Park Rangers

Lawrence Vigouroux
B: Camden, London DOB: 19 November 1993
Academy: Brentford, Tottenham Hotspur
Clubs: Tottenham Hotspur, Hyde United (loan), Liverpool, Swindon Town, Waterford ROI (loan), Everton (Chile), Leyton Orient

Spencer McCall
B: Northwick Park DOB 23/1/1995 D: 21/7/2021
Academy: none
Clubs: Wingate & Finchley, Stevenage FC, Hemel Hempstead Town, Hendon, Harrow Borough, Bishop's Stortford

Beau Amos
B: Hemel Hempstead DOB: 24/06/1995
Academy: Watford
Clubs: Kings Langley

Jack Westlake
B: High Wycombe DOB: 25/10/1994
Academy: Watford
Clubs: Watford, Aylesbury, Chesham United, Tring Athletic,

Mason Bush
B: Welwyn Garden City DOB: 20/1/1995
Academy: Tottenham Hotspur
Clubs: Hemel Hempstead Town, Welwyn Garden City, Kings Langley, Amersham Town

Matt Ball
B: Welwyn Garden City DOB: 26/03/1993
Academy: Norwich City
Clubs: Norwich City, Stevenage FC, Boreham Wood FC, Farnborough FC, Wealdstone FC, St Albans FC, Hendon FC, Biggleswade Town FC

ABOUT THE AUTHOR

Dominic Ball is an English professional footballer who was born in Hertfordshire in 1995 and has played age representative football for both Northern Ireland and England.

Signed by Watford FC's academy as a schoolboy, he later became a youth player with Tottenham Hotspur, where he signed his first professional contract before moving to Rotherham United and onto his current club, Queens Park Rangers.

He has also had loan spells at Cambridge United, Rangers, Peterborough United and Aberdeen.

A rarity in modern football, Dominic successfully studied for an Open University degree in Business Studies which he completed in 2021.

His older brother Matt was also a professional footballer with Norwich City and Stevenage FC and played for several non-League clubs. He now runs a sports management company.

From Winning Teams to Broken Dreams is Dominic's first book, which is intended to provide advice, information and inspiration to future generations of aspiring young footballers.

From Winning Teams to Broken Dreams

Printed in Great Britain
by Amazon

17572967R10108